10
Performance-Based
Projects

Grades 3–5

10

Performance-Based Projects

for the Science Classroom

Todd Stanley

PRUFROCK PRESS INC.
WACO, TEXAS

Prufrock Press Inc.
P.O. Box 8813
Waco, TX 76714-8813
Phone: (800) 998-2208
Fax: (800) 240-0333
http://www.prufrock.com

TABLE OF CONTENTS

INTRODUCTION

Why Project-Based Learning?

Twenty-first century skills, or survival skills, as termed by Tony Wagner in his book *The Global Achievement Gap* (2014), involve students being able to do more than memorize facts and instead apply skills and, more importantly, problem solve (Stoof, Martens, Van Merriënboer, & Bastiaens, 2002). In short, teachers are tasked with the difficult job of trying to create thinkers. This results from businesses complaining that the best and brightest students that the educational system is sending their way are very intelligent but woefully inept at figuring out problems, arguing students know a lot of "facts" but are not "competent" (Bastiaens & Martens, 2000). Any teacher able to help students become these thinkers would be providing them with an advantage when they enter the real world.

The educational system has to do a better job of preparing students to solve real-world problems. How do we do that in the current system of standards and testing? With so much at stake on these achievement tests, the bigger question is: How often in life are we asked to take a pencil-and-paper test? Not very often unless you count online personality quizzes. In real life we are usually dealing with projects, either at work, home, or other settings. If we truly want to get students ready for the real world, we should be teaching them how to handle the real-world dilemma of a project.

As mentioned in *Project-Based Learning for Gifted Students: A Handbook for the 21st-Century Classroom* (Stanley, 2012), according to the Buck

Institute for Education, research studies have demonstrated project-based learning can:

- increase academic achievement on standardized assessment tests;
- teach math, economics, social studies, science, medical skills, and health-related subjects more effectively than traditional teaching methods;
- increase long-term retention of knowledge, skill development, and student and teacher satisfaction;
- prepare students to integrate and explain concepts better than traditional instructional methods;
- prove especially helpful for low-achieving students;
- present a workable model for larger school reform; and
- help students to master 21st-century skills such as communication, independent and critical thinking, and research. (p. 4)

This is why project-based learning is such a good fit for creating such thinkers. It has been discovered that students:

- prefer to structure their own tasks they are working on and establish deadlines as opposed to having the teacher assign them (Dunn, Dunn, & Price 1984; Renzulli, Smith, & Reis 1982; Stewart, 1981);
- learn more and retain content more accurately when allowed to work on projects in which they set the pace (Whitener, 1989);
- show an increased benefit in learning when they teach each other through projects (Kingsley, 1986; Johnsen-Harrris, 1983);
- show improvement in cooperative learning skills when working in groups because they must work together to solve problems (Peterson, 1997); and
- show increased engagement after participating in PBL than students who did not (Grant & Branch, 2005; Horton, Hedetniemi, Wiegert, & Wagner, 2006; Johnston, 2004; Jones & Kalinowski, 2007; Ljung & Blackwell, 1996; McMiller, Lee, Saroop, Green, & Johnson, 2006; Toolin, 2004).

Based on this research, a better question to ask is not why use project-based learning, but rather why not use project-based learning?

What Are the Advantages of Using PBL in a Science Classroom?

Project-based learning is an excellent vehicle to teach 21st-century skills. In *21st-Century Skills: Learning for Life in Our Times* (2009), Bernie Trilling and Charles Fadel mentioned, among valuable 21st-century skills, eight specific skills that PBL can effectively teach:

1. public speaking,
2. problem solving,
3. collaboration,
4. critical thinking,
5. information literacy,
6. creativity,
7. adaptability, and
8. self-direction. (p. viii)

Science lends itself to the skills of creativity and adaptability. Creativity involves outside-the-box thinking. When you think about the greatest outside-the-box thinkers, you might consider Leonardo da Vinci, Albert Einstein, or Stephen Hawking—all of them scientists. How much of an outside-the-box thinker must one be to propose that the sun is the center of the universe when other scientific experts placed the Earth at its center? Or how creative was the individual who suggested that man evolved from apes even though the popular doctrine was more divine? As radical and preposterous their thinking was in their times, Copernicus's and Charles Darwin's theories are now accepted as scientific fact. It took these men questioning what they had been told and being creative enough to think of better solutions. How creative are today's scientists who are able to create computers that fit in the palm of your hand or cars that run on electricity? Creative writers can imagine all the crazy, outside-the-box ideas they want—but these are just words. Scientists actually create these advancements. How many ideas from Jules Verne's imagination became reality due to a scientist creating it, including the submarine, videoconferencing, and the Taser gun? Without the creativity of scientific minds, we would probably still be living in caves, but some creative individual figured out how to use fire—and the world has never been the same.

You might wonder how students can use creativity in the science classroom. Are they not just learning facts that someone else was creative enough to discover? How much creativity can be used in learning the elements or knowing the three stages of the rock cycle? How outside-the-box can one get while learning about different types of clouds or the states of matter? The nonscientific answer—plenty. In the science classroom, students need the chance to be innovative and creative. After all, the very nature of science is questioning and thinking outside of the box. And being able to think creatively is essential to students' futures. The U.S. Department of Labor lists the two fastest-growing occupations as biomedical engineers and network systems and data communications analysts. Both of these careers require workers who can be innovative and think creatively (Haines, 2011).

Just looking at the Next Generation Science Standards (NGSS), employed by more than half of the states, one can see that creativity will be needed to master many skills:

- 3-LS1-1. Develop models to describe that organisms have unique and diverse life cycles but all have in common birth, growth, reproduction, and death.
- 3-LS2-1. Construct an argument that some animals form groups that help members survive.
- 3-ESS3-1. Make a claim about the merit of a design solution that reduces the impacts of a weather-related hazard.
- 4-PS3-4. Apply scientific ideas to design, test, and refine a device that converts energy from one form to another.
- 4-PS4-2. Develop a model to describe that light reflecting from objects and entering the eye allows objects to be seen.
- 4-PS4-3. Generate and compare multiple solutions that use patterns to transfer information.
- 5-PS1-1. Develop a model to describe that matter is made of particles too small to be seen.
- 3-5-ETS1-1. Define a simple design problem reflecting a need or a want that includes specified criteria for success and constraints on materials, time, or cost.

Science also relies on adaptability. If you need proof of its importance, look no further than Thomas Edison, one of the greatest inventors and scientists of all time. Some of his inventions include the motion picture camera, phonograph, and the mimeograph. Arguably his greatest invention was the incandescent light bulb. While testing his experiment, Edison went through various materials to use as its filament. He tried platinum, but that was too expensive. Carbon burned up too easily. He used carbonized sewing thread, but the bulb would not last more than a day. Finally, while fanning himself on an especially hot day, he unwound a thread of bamboo from the oriental fan he was using. He carbonized it and experimented with it as a filament—and history was rewritten. When asked about his attempts, Edison was quoted as saying, "I didn't fail 1,000 times. The light bulb was an invention with 1,000 steps." Through trial and error, he showed immense adaptability—a necessary skill when using the scientific method.

The scientific method has six steps:
1. **Purpose:** State the problem.
2. **Research:** Find out about the topic.
3. **Hypothesis:** Predict the outcome to the problem.
4. **Experiment:** Test your hypothesis.
5. **Analysis:** Record the results of the experiment.
6. **Conclusion:** Compare the outcome of the experiment with the hypothesis.

Scientists start with a hypothesis and must conduct an experiment to prove whether it is true or not. More often than not, the experiment does not result in the way a scientist hoped, so he or she has to adapt the hypothesis and try again. If a scientist is not adaptable, it will be very difficult to succeed, because as soon as he or she hits a roadblock, he or she will be stopped. Scientists need to be able to adapt their thinking and their experiments for the greater good of scientific discovery.

Some of the NGSS that require students to be adaptable include:
- 3-PS2-1. Plan and conduct an investigation to provide evidence of the effects of balanced and unbalanced forces on the motion of an object.
- 3-LS3-1. Analyze and interpret data to provide evidence that plants and animals have traits inherited from parents and that variation of these traits exists in a group of similar organisms.
- 4-PS3-3. Ask questions and predict outcomes about the changes in energy that occur when objects collide.
- 4-ESS3-2. Generate and compare multiple solutions to reduce the impacts of natural Earth processes on humans.
- 5-PS1-4. Conduct an investigation to determine whether the mixing of two or more substances results in new substances.

- 5-ESS3-1. Obtain and combine information about ways individual communities use science ideas to protect the Earth's resources and environment.
- 3-5-ETS1-3. Plan and carry out fair tests in which variables are controlled and failure points are considered to identify aspects of a model or prototype that can be improved.

The projects in this book will allow your students to be both creative and adaptable. The better students become at these skills, the more valuable the skills will be in real-world situations.

What Sorts of Products Could Be Used in a Science Classroom?

As laid out in *Performance-Based Assessment for 21st-Century Skills* (Stanley, 2014), there are 10 different types of assessments that can be used in a project-based learning environment:

1. oral presentations,
2. debates/speeches,
3. role playing,
4. group discussions,
5. interviews,
6. portfolios,
7. exhibitions,
8. essays,
9. research papers, and
10. journals/student logs. (p. 43)

There are, of course, many other types, but these are the 10 this book will be focusing on and providing examples of.

Keep in mind these project plans can be changed, added to, rearranged, and anything else you need to do to make them effective for your students. There are some that contain lessons that could be used for other projects, so move aspects around and set them up the way that works best for your students.

1 Oral Presentation

Much of what a student knows can be expressed in an oral presentation. Classrooms are full of the type of student who raises his hand and can provide insightful, meaningful responses when taking part in discussion, but as soon as you ask that same student to write down his thoughts, you are lucky to get a one- or two-word written response. He is not able, or more likely, not willing, to give you the same insightful responses in writing. In dealing with these kinds of students, the question for me became: Why couldn't this student provide his answers orally, especially if it meant getting responses like he did in class? On the flip side are those students who do not know how to express themselves in an oral presentation, and the acquisition of the skill is very valuable to them.

What It Looks Like

Oral presentations can take several forms, but they typically consist of an informative speech designed to educate an audience. Some of the forms can be:

- an individual or group report,
- an oral briefing,
- an oral exam,
- a panel discussion, or
- an oral critique.

The student's goal in an oral presentation is to verbally teach classmates or the audience what she has learned after researching a particular topic or skill. A successful oral presentation needs to be set up just like an essay would, with a topic sentence, supporting details, and several drafts before the final presentation. This structure is something that should be taught to students. This can be done with modeling, looking at exemplary examples of great oral presentations, or practicing presentations with no consequences.

Survival of the Fittest

Plants and animals have both internal and external structures that allow them to survive. In this project, students will research and study a specific plant or animal, looking at what internal and external structures it has that allow it to survive and grow, and how those structures affect behavior and reproduction. They will then present their findings to the class.

Connections to NGSS

- 4-LS1-1

Materials

- Project Outline: Survival of the Fittest (student copies)
- Suggested Timeline
- Lesson: What Helps Organisms Survive?
- Lesson: Conducting Research
- Lesson: What Makes a Good Presentation?
- Handout 1.1: Internet Scavenger Hunt (student copies)
- Handout 1.2: Researching Your Topic (student copies)
- Handout 1.3: Organism Graphic Organizer (student copies)
- Handout 1.4: What Makes a Good Presentation? (student copies)
- Handout 1.5: Peer Review (student copies)
- Product Rubric (student copies)

Name: _____ Date: _____

PROJECT OUTLINE

Survival of the Fittest

Directions: Plants and animals have both internal and external structures that allow them to survive. For example, porcupines have external quills that protect them from predators, and cacti store water internally to survive in harsh desert climates.

You will research and study a specific plant or animal, looking at what internal and external structures it has that allow it to survive and grow, and how those structures affect behavior and reproduction. You will then present your findings to the class. Consider one of the following animals or plants as your topic.

Animals

- Penguin
- Camel
- Bear
- Frog
- Koala
- Peppered Moth
- Scarlet Kingsnake
- Brown Booby
- Meerkat
- Aye-Aye

- Apple Snail
- Gerenuk
- Fish Hook Ant
- Amazonian Flycatcher
- Sandgrouse
- Roadrunner
- Scorpion
- Kangaroo
- Leaf-Tailed Gecko

Plants

- Venus Fly Trap
- Cactus
- Dandelion
- Prairie Shrub
- Epiphyte Orchid
- Water Lily
- Sunflower
- Euphorbia

- Liana
- Bromeliad
- Nepenthes
- Purple Saxifrage
- Arctic Poppy
- Neem
- Mangrove
- Duckweed

© **Prufrock Press Inc.** • *10 Performance-Based Projects for the Science Classroom*
This page may be photocopied or reproduced with permission for single classroom use only.

Project 1: Oral Presentation

SUGGESTED TIMELINE

DAY				
1 Introduce the project and conduct Lesson: What Helps Organisms Survive?	**2** Conduct Lesson: Conducting Research (see Handout 1.1, Handout 1.2).	**3** Have students begin researching their topics (see Handout 1.3).	**4** Have students continue researching their topics.	**5** Have students continue researching their topics.
6 Have students continue researching their topics.	**7** Have students continue researching their topics.	**8** Conduct Lesson: What Makes a Good Presentation? (see Handout 1.4).	**9** Have students practice their presentations.	**10** Have students practice their presentations.
11 Have students conduct peer reviews (see Handout 1.5).	**12** Begin student presentations (see Product Rubric).	**13** Continue student presentations.	**14** Continue student presentations.	**15** Continue student presentations.

What Helps Organisms Survive?

What about the internal and external structure of humans allows them to survive, grow, behave, and reproduce? Discuss the following facts about humans with students, noting that they will soon be researching the characteristics of an organism of their choosing.

Human Characteristics

Survival
What about this organism's features, inside and out, allows it to survive in its environment?

Internal Characteristics:	External Characteristics:
<ul><li>**Brain:** Receives and sends signals to other organs through the nervous system and through secreted hormones; responsible for thoughts, feelings, memory storage, etc.</li><li>**Heart:** Responsible for pumping blood throughout the body</li><li>**Kidneys:** Remove waste and extra fluid from the blood</li><li>**Liver:** Detoxes harmful chemicals, breaks down drugs, filters blood, secretes and produces blood-clotting proteins</li><li>**Lungs:** Remove oxygen from air and transfer it to blood where it can be sent to cells</li></ul>	<ul><li>**Opposable Thumbs:** Allow humans to work with tools in ways other organisms are not able to</li><li>**Hair:** Provides protection from the elements (sun, cold, heat)</li><li>**Standing Erect:** Allows humans to travel and explore new territories, see farther than they can smell, see danger better, and use tools because hands are free</li></ul>

Growth	
What about the rate of growth, size, or development of this organism allows it to survive?	
Internal Characteristics: ◆ **Organs:** Grow with humans as they are developing ◆ **Knowledge:** Humans become smarter as they age, though the brain may not be physically growing	External Characteristics: ◆ **Life Expectancy:** Increased over centuries with increased medical knowledge ◆ **Size:** Human bodies grow until they reach a limit
Behavior	
What about the behavior of this organism, both internally (might not even be voluntary) and externally, allows it to survive better?	
Internal Characteristics: ◆ **Fight or Flight:** Protects from threats ◆ **Immune System:** Fights infection and illness, heals the body when wounded	External Characteristics: ◆ **Superiority:** Humans act as if they are the planet's superior organisms ◆ **Technology:** Has made lives and survival easier
Reproduction	
What about this organism's reproduction methods supports its survival?	
Internal Characteristics: ◆ **Females:** Carry eggs and embryos inside their bodies ◆ **Males:** Fertilize the female eggs ◆ **Gestation:** Time from fertilization to birth is typically 9 months	External Characteristics: ◆ **Physical Attributes:** Certain attributes (attractiveness, fitness, eye color) attract humans to each other ◆ **Other External Attributes:** Certain attributes that are not physical (job, salary) attract humans to each other

Conducting Research

Tell students that they can find almost anything on the Internet, which means they will always have to go through a lot of information that might not be relevant to their topic.

There are various search engines to help them find information, such as:

- ◆ Google (http://www.google.com),
- ◆ Yahoo (http://www.yahoo.com), and
- ◆ Bing (http://www.bing.com).

When they search, they will want to:

- ◆ be as specific as possible without being too specific (e.g., too general = "airplanes," too specific = "paper airplanes with cool decals");
- ◆ narrow their search without eliminating sites because they do not contain the exact wording; and
- ◆ not just use the first website they encounter (i.e., just because it comes up in a search does not mean it is what they are looking for).

Distribute Handout 1.1: Internet Scavenger Hunt. Tell students to imagine they are writing a report about dogs. If they Google the term "dog," they retrieve more than 853,000,000 results. That's more than anyone can possibly go through. How do they refine their search? The scavenger hunt will show them how.

Have students select their research topics and distribute Handout 1.2: Researching Your Topic.

What Makes a Good Presentation?

There are certain elements that make up a good oral presentation. Distribute Handout 1.4: What Makes a Good Presentation? and review the 10 things for students to consider:

1. Keep consistent eye contact.
2. Use a strong, confident voice.
3. Avoid "umms," "ahhhs," and "likes."
4. Keep your hands in the correct place. (Don't put them in your pockets or cross your arms.)
5. Don't read your information. Present it.
6. Show you care about your topic. (Don't use a monotone voice.)
7. Stand up straight.
8. Be prepared. (Practice ahead of time.)
9. Maintain professionalism. (Don't giggle or say inappropriate things.)
10. Have a flow to your presentation. (Have notes to fall back on if you get stuck.)

Have students watch an example of a good oral presentation. Good examples include:

- TED Talks
- Dr. Martin Luther King Jr.'s "I Have a Dream Speech"
- Infomercials
- John Green Nerdfighters Presentations
- Book talks on YouTube

Have students listen and go through the list on Handout 1.4, identifying whether or not the presenter met all of the requirements of a good presentation.

Name: _____ Date: _____

Internet Scavenger Hunt

Directions: Use a search engine to answer the following questions.

1. How many hits do you get when you search the term "dog"?

2. How many hits do you receive when you refine your search to "dog breeds"?

3. How many hits do you receive when you refine your search to "kid-friendly dog breeds"?

4. If you are trying to find out which of these dogs is the largest, what key term could you use to refine your search even more?

5. Using one of the three search engines, determine which breed is the most popular in the United States.

Project 1: Oral Presentation

Handout 1.1: Internet Scavenger Hunt, *continued*

6. How many different breeds of dog are there in the world?

7. What is the definition of an "occiput"?

8. What special membrane allows a dog to see at night?

9. Go to http://www.westminsterkennelclub.org. Under "About WKC" in the top banner, click on "Records." Click on "Best In Show Winners" and find out the breed of dog that won in 1972.

10. Go to http://www.whole-dog-journal.com. In the search bar, which is indicated by a blue magnifying glass, type in "Dalmatian" to see what year the article on low uric acid was written.

HANDOUT 1.2

Researching Your Topic

Directions: When you are conducting research, you should consider the following five steps.

Step 1: Construct Research Questions

Write specific questions. Doing so will help you narrow your topic and determine exactly what information you need. Sample questions:

- How many breeds of dog are there?
- What is the most popular breed of dog?
- How did dogs come to be domesticated?
- What breed makes the best therapy dogs?
- How many dogs are there in the United States?
- Where is the largest population of dogs found?
- What breed is responsible for the most attacks?

Step 2: Figure Out Possible Sources of Information

Before going online, try to identify any sources that might have information on your topic. For example, you might list:

- American Humane Association
- American Society for Prevention of Cruelty to Animals
- American Kennel Club
- Westminster Kennel Club
- YouTube (might have documentaries on dogs and various breeds)

Step 3: Identify Keywords

Review the questions and sources you brainstormed in Steps 1–2, and circle the keywords. What is it specifically you want to find? Use this to refine your search.

Handout 1.2: Researching Your Topic, *continued*

Step 4: Get Ready To Search

You're finally ready to choose a tool(s) and begin your search. Depending on the time you have and your own personal preference, you can start with a search engine, or a specific site of your own choice.

If you are using a search engine, you will want to use the keywords you identified in Step 3 to develop your search query. The trick is to try several combinations of keywords. Remember—there's no one *right* way to conduct research online. Just be sure to start with a strategy and experiment with different search tools to get the best results.

Step 5: Finding Easy-to-Understand, School-Appropriate Sites

Adding a simple suffix to your search may result in more student-appropriate, student-friendly results. For instance, add the following to your refine your search:

- ... for kids
- ... for students
- ... for children
- ... for school

These will make the hits you receive from your search more age-appropriate and easier to understand because you will be the audience they are written for.

HANDOUT 1.3

Organism Graphic Organizer

Directions: Use this graphic organizer to list your organism's external and internal characteristics that affect its survival, growth, behavior, and reproduction.

Survival	
What about this organism's features, inside and out, allows it to survive in its environment?	
Internal Characteristics:	External Characteristics:

Growth	
What about the rate of growth, size, or development of this organism allows it to survive?	
Internal Characteristics:	External Characteristics:

Project 1: Oral Presentation

Handout 1.3: Organism Graphic Organizer, *continued*

Behavior
What about the behavior of this organism, both internally (might not even be voluntary) and externally, allows it to survive better?

Internal Characteristics:	External Characteristics:

Reproduction
What about this organism's reproduction methods supports its survival?

Internal Characteristics:	External Characteristics:

HANDOUT 1.4

What Makes a Good Presentation?

Directions: There are certain elements that make up a good oral presentation. Here are 10 things to consider:

1. Keep consistent eye contact.

2. Use a strong, confident voice.

3. Avoid "umms," "ahhhs," and "likes."

4. Keep your hands in the correct place. (Don't put them in your pockets or cross your arms.)

5. Don't read your information. Present it.

6. Show you care about your topic. (Don't use a monotone voice.)

7. Stand up straight.

8. Be prepared. (Practice ahead of time.)

9. Maintain professionalism. (Don't giggle or say inappropriate things.)

10. Have a flow to your presentation. (Have notes to fall back on if you get stuck.)

Project 1: Oral Presentation

Name: _____ Date: _____

HANDOUT 1.5

Peer Review

Directions: Circle whether your peer did or did not do each of the following.

Peer's Name: _____

Peer's Topic: _____

1. He or she kept consistent eye contact.   Yes   No

2. He or she used a strong, confident voice.   Yes   No

3. He or she did not use "umms," "ahhhs," and "likes."   Yes   No

4. He or she used his or her hands correctly (not in his or her   Yes   No
   pockets or arms crossed).

5. He or she presented his or her information; he or she did   Yes   No
   not read it.

6. He or she cares about his or her topic (no monotone voice).   Yes   No

7. He or she stood up straight.   Yes   No

8. He or she was prepared (practiced ahead of time).   Yes   No

9. He or she maintained professionalism (no giggling or   Yes   No
   saying inappropriate things).

10. His or her presentation flowed (and he or she had notes to   Yes   No
    fall back on if he or she got stuck).

Project 1: Oral Presentation

Name: _____ Date: _____

Survival of the Fittest

Animal/Plant: _____

Overall	Presentation	Content
Excellent (A)	◆ Presenter spoke clearly and slowly and could be heard the entire time. ◆ Presenter's demeanor was professional, and it sounded as though he or she rehearsed several times. ◆ Presentation was organized in a manner that made it easy to follow and understand.	◆ Presenter provided several examples to illustrate both internal and external structures. ◆ Presenter provided lots of detail when talking about the internal/external structures, displaying a level of understanding. ◆ Presenter discussed how the animal/plant has internal/external structures that allow it to survive, grow, behave, and reproduce.
Good (B–C)	◆ Presenter spoke clearly and slowly but was difficult to hear once or twice. ◆ Presenter's demeanor was professional throughout much of the presentation but lacked at times, and it sounded like he or she rehearsed but could have used more practice. ◆ Presentation was organized in a manner that made it easy to follow and understand, but there were a couple of instances where it was difficult to follow.	◆ Presenter provided examples to illustrate both internal and external structures but could use more. ◆ Presenter provided lots of detail when talking about the internal/external structures, displaying a level of understanding. ◆ Presenter discussed how the animal/plant has internal/external structures that allow it to survive, grow, behave, and reproduce.
Needs Improvement (D–F)	◆ Presenter could not be heard for a good portion and/or did not speak slowly and clearly. ◆ Presenter's demeanor was not professional throughout much of the presentation, causing a distraction, and it did not sound as though he or she rehearsed. ◆ Presentation was not very organized, making it difficult to follow and understand.	◆ Presenter did not provide any or very few examples that illustrate both internal and external structures. ◆ Presenter did not provide much detail when talking about the internal/external structures, lacking a level of understanding. ◆ Presenter did not explain two or more of the topics (survive, grow, behave, and reproduce).

Project 1: Oral Presentation

2 Debate/Speech

This is another form of oral presentation, but instead of seeking to inform, the main goal is to persuade. Debates and speeches are a higher level of thinking because they don't just convey information but employ tactics to convince someone that one student's opinions or viewpoints are more valuable than another's. It is a process more complicated than the usual presentation because it looks at "ethos, the credibility of the speaker; logos, the logical proof and reasoning presented in the words of the speech; and pathos, the use of emotional appeals to influence the audience" (Brydon & Scott, 2000).

What It Looks Like

Debates are especially great to use when the concept being taught is ambiguous or allows for multiple perspectives. Speeches are another form of this persuasive oral presentation. While delivering a speech, the student is either playing a role or representing a organization. He must convince people of his platform or ideals. Although not as interactive as a debate, the speech still requires the student to tap into higher levels of thinking and make a sound argument.

Biome in a Biodome

In this project, students will work in groups of five to create an ecosystem for a biodome. They will decide the features of the ecosystem, as well as the organisms that inhabit it. They must select organisms—producers, decomposers, herbivores, omnivores, and carnivores. Each must be from a different ecosystem and must allow the ecosystem to maintain itself over a number of years. They will develop a model of their biodome and present it to a panel, justifying their decisions. The panel will then take counterpoints from the audience and decide which proposal they believe will be the most successful.

Connections to NGSS

- 5-LS2-1

Materials

- Project Outline: Biome in a Biodome (student copies)
- Suggested Timeline
- Lesson: What Is an Ecosystem?
- Lesson: Roles in an Ecosystem
- Lesson: Different Types of Ecosystems
- Lesson: Creating an Argument
- Handout 2.1: Exploring Ecosystems (student copies)
- Handout 2.2: Ecosystem for Biome (student copies)
- Handout 2.3: Creating an Argument (student copies)
- Product Rubric (student copies)

PROJECT OUTLINE

Biome in a Biodome

Directions: You will work in a group of five to create an ecosystem for a biodome. A biodome is a closed ecological system created by man. You will decide the features of the ecosystem, as well as the organisms that inhabit it. You must select organisms—producers, decomposers, herbivores, omnivores, and carnivores. Each must be from a different ecosystem and must allow the ecosystem to maintain itself over a number of years.

You will develop a model of your biodome and present it to a panel, justifying your decisions. You need to include an argument for why you are choosing the organisms you are and how they will help sustain the ecosystem. You will also need to discuss the challenges of having organisms from different ecosystems. The panel will then take counterpoints from the audience and decide which proposal they believe will be the most successful.

You and your group members will take on the following roles:

♦ **Producer:** Responsible for keeping everyone on task (provides energy for everyone).
♦ **Carnivore:** Responsible for the research (the meat of the project).
♦ **Herbivore:** Responsible for writing the speech (the vegetables of the project).
♦ **Omnivore:** Responsible for creating the model (have to balance the meat with the vegetables).
♦ **Decomposer:** Responsible for checking everyone's work (cleans up any messes left behind).

Creating Your Model

You will need to find a way to demonstrate what the biome looks like and how the organisms you have chosen will coexist with one another. The level and complexity of your model is completely up to you, provided you demonstrate the movement of matter among plants, animals, decomposers, and the environment. Some suggestions include:

♦ using an aquarium to house your biome,
♦ making it with a shoebox,
♦ constructing it with Legos or other building blocks,
♦ designing it on a poster,
♦ creating a computer simulation, or
♦ building it with wood.

SUGGESTED TIMELINE

DAY				
1 Introduce the project and conduct Lesson: What Is an Ecosystem?	**2** Conduct Lesson: Roles in an Ecosystem (see Handout 2.1).	**3** Conduct Lesson: Different Types of Ecosystems.	**4** Have students form groups and begin researching ecosystems (see Handout 2.2).	**5** Have students continue researching ecosystems and begin selecting their organisms.
6 Have students continue researching ecosystems and selecting their organisms.	**7** Have students continue researching ecosystems and selecting their organisms.	**8** Conduct Lesson: Creating an Argument (see Handout 2.3).	**9** Have groups create their arguments.	**10** Have groups finalize their arguments.
11 Have groups begin creating their model.	**12** Have groups continue creating their model.	**13** Have groups continue creating their model.	**14** Have groups complete creating their model.	**15** Have groups present their model to panel and justify choices (see Product Rubric).

LESSON

What Is an Ecosystem?

Tell students that an ecosystem includes all of the living things (plants, animals, and organisms) in a specific area, interacting with each other and also with their environments (weather, earth, sun, soil, climate, atmosphere). These organisms work together in an ecosystem, and if any one of them is affected, it affects the entire ecosystem.

Ask: *A wooded area could be an ecosystem. What sorts of animals would you find in a wooded area?* Possible answers:

- Squirrels
- Birds
- Deer
- Raccoons

These are known as the population. But there are other organisms in a wooded area. Ask: *And what do these organisms eat?* Possible answers:

- **Squirrels:** Nuts
- **Birds:** Worms, insects
- **Deer:** Plants
- **Raccoons:** Fish, smaller mammals

Ask: *And what do the organisms they eat have to eat?*

- **Nuts:** Sunlight, water, soil
- **Worms, insects:** Soil, plants
- **Plants:** Sunlight, water, soil
- **Fish, smaller mammals:** Smaller organisms, plants

Tell students: *Each one of these organisms has a specific role in the ecosystem called a* niche *in order to provide energy to the ecosystem. If you take any of them away, it affects everything else in the ecosystem. For example, what would happen to our wooded ecosystem if someone came in and bulldozed all the trees to put in a housing development? What would be lost? Not only might food be lost for the squirrels, but what about where they live or where the birds live? This is their* habitat *that is affected.*

Tell students a *biome* is a larger area for an ecosystem that contains similar organisms and has similar weather. Take out wooded area and make it a forest. What sort of weather is typical to a biome that supports a forest? Different forests have different sorts of weather and thus are different types of biomes:

- **Rain forest:** Tropical weather, lots of rain
- **Deciduous forest:** Seasons change but rain is present
- **Coniferous forest:** Seasons change but typically is a colder climate

Because the *climate* is different, different sorts of organisms live there—those that can survive and thrive in each climate.

LESSON

Roles in an Ecosystem

Distribute Handout 2.1: Exploring Ecosystems and review the terms from the last lesson. Then, discuss organisms' roles in an ecosystem, providing students with several examples, such as the following wooded ecosystem:

- ◆ **Producer—Acorn tree:** Gets nutrients from the ground produced by decomposers
- ◆ **Herbivore—Squirrel:** Eats the nuts from the tree
- ◆ **Omnivore—Raccoon:** Eats the squirrel as well as plants
- ◆ **Carnivore—Wolf:** Eats the raccoon and squirrel
- ◆ **Decomposer—Maggots:** Eat the dead body of wolf, squirrel, and raccoon

Tell students that in an ecosystem, each organism works to provide food for other organisms. It looks like a big circle. Everyone in the ecosystem is eating everyone else. Someone has someone else or even multiple organisms to eat. Everyone plays a specific part. Thus, if you take one of the organisms out of the ecosystem or affect their habitat, it can affect the entire ecosystem because that food source is no longer available to others. So, if in the example, there was a drought that wiped out the trees in the wooded area, it would affect the squirrels directly by taking away their food source. It would also affect the others.

Activity

Using the members of the wooded ecosystem, manipulate in groups or as a class each of these organisms and where they fit on the food chain. Then, draw how the transfer of energy occurs throughout this food chain.

Different Types of Ecosystems

Tell students that because there are so many different climates in the world, there are lots of different ecosystems. Certain animals can live in those biomes and certain ones cannot. For example, a fish cannot live on land, and a squirrel cannot live in the ocean. There are also animals that cannot handle high temperatures and cannot live in the desert, and animals with thin coats of fur that could not survive in the arctic. Ask: *What are some different types of ecosystems you know of?*

Generate a list of ecosystems on the board. Choose five or six of these. Divide students into groups of five. Have each group research one of the ecosystems and the organisms in it.

Land Ecosystems

- Desert
- Grassland
- Taiga
- Tropical rainforest
- Deciduous forest
- Tundra
- Savanna
- Urban
- Agroecosystem
- Prairie

Water Ecosystems

- River
- Wetland
- Coral reef
- Deep sea
- Marsh
- Ocean
- Lake

Creating an Argument

Tell students that when trying to convince a group of people to accept their point of view, they should consider the 6 Ps. Distribute and discuss Handout 2.3: Creating an Argument.

1. **Prepare:** Make sure you know what you are talking about. You can do this by knowing everything there is to know about your topic, so that if things do not go as planned or you are asked questions, you have the knowledge to construct additional arguments. Having notes and points to refer to will be helpful when you get stuck.

2. **Prioritize:** Be sure to stress the important aspects of your argument. Why did you make the choices you did? What makes this choice better than another choice? What advantages does your choice provide? Prioritizing also means finishing with your strongest argument. Nothing hurts an argument more than just trailing off when finished or simply stating "that's all." Finish your argument with something that will make your audience remember it.

3. **Pivot:** This means going back and forth between why your argument is the best choice and making counterarguments why the other choice might not be the best one. By pivoting back and forth, you may answer audience members' questions.

4. **Present:** Although you should prepare your speech ahead of time, try not to read it to your audience. You need to present your ideas as though you care about them and believe they are the best choices. If you read your remarks in a monotone voice, why should the audience care?

5. **Persuade:** Do you make a convincing argument for choosing your side by providing detail and examples that allow the audience to see your point of view? Do you provide an anecdote that proves your point and helps others to experience your side?

6. **Presentable:** Anything you can do to convince your audience of your perspective can and should be used. Part of this is the way you present yourself. Are you dressed in a professional manner or a manner conducive to your argument? Do you stand up straight, avoid putting your hands in your pockets, avoid using "ums" and "likes," and present yourself in a confident way? The littlest things can win or lose an argument.

HANDOUT 2.1

Exploring Ecosystems

Directions: Make sure you understand these terms and the roles in the ecosystem while creating your own.

Ecosystem Terms

- **Ecosystem:** All of the living and nonliving things in an area
- **Population:** A group of organisms of one species that live in an area at the same time
- **Biome:** A large ecosystem with generally the same climate and organisms
- **Niche:** A role an organism has in an ecosystem
- **Habitat:** The place in which an organism lives

Roles in an Ecosystem

Because every organism in the ecosystem works together to sustain it, each organism has a very specific task as part of the ecosystem. There are five major roles in an ecosystem.

- **Producer:** An organism that makes organic nutrients that are transferred to consumers when eaten. Typically are plants, trees, grass, etc.
- **Herbivore:** An animal that eats just plants, a vegetarian. They get their energy from plants, nuts, grass, etc. Most of them do not have the correct teeth or digestive tracts to eat meat.
- **Omnivore:** An animal that eats both animals and plants. This organism can eat either one depending on the supply/availability of the organism as well as desire.
- **Carnivore:** An animal that eats other animals only, a meat eater. They have teeth (fangs, incisors) designed to chew meat, as well as digestive tracts that allow them to break down the meat into energy.
- **Decomposer:** An organism that breaks down remains of dead organisms, releasing the inorganic compounds back into the environment for reuse. Because everything dies, there needs to be a way to transfer the dead material into energy. Decomposers help do this. Can be as small as bacteria, a worm/maggot, or fungi.

Name: _____ Date: _____

Ecosystem for Biome

Directions: Use this graphic organizer to record your research while searching for possible candidates for your ecosystem.

Ecosystem Role	Candidates	Biome Resident
Decomposer		
Carnivore		
Omnivore		
Herbivore		
Producer		

Name: _____ Date: _____

HANDOUT 2.3

Creating an Argument

Directions: When creating an argument, consider the six Ps.

1. **Prepare:** Make sure you know what you are talking about.

2. **Prioritize:** Stress the important aspects of your argument.

3. **Pivot:** Go back and forth between why your argument is the best choice and counterarguments about why the other choice(s) might not be the best.

4. **Present:** Discuss your ideas as though you care about them and believe they are the best choices.

5. **Persuade:** Make a convincing argument for choosing your side by providing detail and examples that allow the audience to see your point of view.

6. **Presentable:** Dress in a professional manner or a manner conducive to your argument.

Project 2: Debate/Speech

PRODUCT RUBRIC

Biome in a Biodome

Overall	Presentation	Content	Model
Excellent (A)	• Presentation can be clearly heard the entire time and the participants speak slowly and clearly. • Presenters' demeanors are professional throughout the entire presentation. It sounds as though it has been rehearsed several times. • Presentation is organized in a manner that makes it easy to follow and understand.	• Students provide several logical examples to illustrate why they chose the organisms they did. • Students provide lots of detail when talking about their ecosystem, showing a level of understanding. • Students are persuasive in their arguments, using several techniques to sway the audience as to why their choices are the best.	• Model clearly demonstrates the movement of matter among plants, animals, decomposers, and the environment. • Model is professional-looking, bringing the biome to life. • Model is clearly explained, all parts being discussed in detail and the reasons for inclusion of various features.
Good (B–C)	• Presentation can be clearly heard for most of the time and the participants speak slowly and clearly, but there are a couple of parts where it is difficult to hear. • Presenters' demeanors are professional throughout much of the presentation, but there are times when they lack professionalism. It sounds rehearsed but could have used more practice. • Presentation is organized in a manner that makes it easy to follow and understand, but a few parts are difficult to follow.	• Students provide examples to illustrate why they chose the organisms they did but do not always make a convincing argument. • Students provide details when talking about their ecosystem, but do not always seem to show a level of understanding. • Students are persuasive in their arguments, using a technique(s) to sway the audience, but they are not always convincing.	• Model demonstrates the movement of matter among plants, animals, decomposers, and the environment, but is not always clear or leaves one out. • Model looks like a good school project, giving those viewing it a basic idea of what this biome would look like. • Model is explained, but all of the reasons for inclusion of various features are not discussed.

© **Prufrock Press Inc.** • *10 Performance-Based Projects for the Science Classroom*

Project 2: Debate/Speech

Name: _____ Date: _____

Product Rubric: Biome in a Biodome, *continued*

Overall	Presentation	Content	Model
Needs Work (D–F)	◆ Presentation cannot be heard for a good portion and/or the participants do not speak slowly and clearly. ◆ Presenters' demeanors are not professional throughout much of the presentation, causing distraction. It does not sound as though it was rehearsed. ◆ The presentation is not very organized, making it difficult to follow and understand.	◆ Students do not provide many examples to illustrate why they chose the organisms they did. ◆ Students do not provide enough detail when talking about their ecosystem, showing a lack of understanding. ◆ Students are not persuasive in their arguments, failing to choose techniques to sway the audience.	◆ Model does not demonstrate the movement of matter among plants, animals, decomposers, and the environment. ◆ Model looks like it was thrown together without much thought, leaving those viewing it to wonder what it represents. ◆ Model is not explained, causing confusion on how the biome is set up and why.

© **Prufrock Press Inc.** • *10 Performance-Based Projects for the Science Classroom***

Project 2: Debate/Speech

3 Group Discussion

Discussions can take what is being learned to a higher level. There are two types of group discussions. One involves students participating and answering with very surface-level responses. The discussion dies on the vine before it can bloom. It looks like a discussion, but it certainly does not feel like one. There is usually no energy, no passion, and, although you might get the information you seek from students, no depth. The second type of group discussion is one in which students cannot wait to participate because what they want to share is burning a hole in their minds. It may require some content knowledge, but it also requires tapping into experiences and opinions. This is the type of discussion you want to have in your classroom.

What It Looks Like

An easy way to make a group discussion meaningful is to make sure the questions being asked are higher level questions. If you are looking for discussions to generate close-ended, knowledge-based information, it becomes a hunt-and-peck event, where you are simply looking for someone to provide the correct answer. If, however, the questions are open-ended, higher level questions designed to be cracked open and explored, the discussion will be meaningful. Some of this involves preparing challenging, higher level questions ahead of time. This also means being able to generate these higher level questions in response to what a student has said. It requires a teacher to be able to think quickly on her feet and ask appropriate follow-up questions to mine all of the meaningful lessons from a conversation.

Group discussions do not need to be led by the teacher. Teachers often feel the need to be the ones steering the ship so that it will head in the direction they want it to go, but sometimes the most interesting trips involve detours. In this case, allowing the discussion to wander to seemingly unrelated topics or to allow students to explore ideas you had not even considered might actually produce better results than you expect. Dividing the students into groups and providing them with a few guiding questions to get the discussion going can lead to these results. Without the teacher there, students might provide more creative answers instead of searching for the answer they believe the teacher is looking for.

Grading a discussion can be a little challenging, but taking copious notes on how a student responds and his level of understanding, or even recording the discussion for you to go back to later are methods you can use to assess a discussion.

How Can We Save the Planet?

Science can be used to save the planet. In this project, students will work in groups of four to research and propose a scientific idea that will help the community protect the Earth's resources and environment. They will need to determine the cost and implementation of such a program, as well as how to communicate it to the community. Each group will then present to a panel of influential members of the community, discussing why its option is the most realistic and affordable for the community.

Connections to NGSS

- 5-ESS3-1

Materials

- Project Outline: How Can We Save the Planet? (student copies)
- Suggested Timeline

- Lesson: Can You Make a Difference?
- Lesson: Developing a Proposal
- Handout 3.1: Developing a Proposal (student copies)
- Teacher-Led Discussion Assessment Form (teacher's copies)
- Group Discussion Assessment Form (teacher's copies)
- Student-Led Discussion Assessment Form (teacher's copies)
- Product Rubric (student copies)

Supplemental Materials

- Documentary about protecting the environment
- Authentic audience for students to present to (local officials, parents, or other class, etc.)

Name: _____ Date: _____

PROJECT OUTLINE

How Can We Save the Planet?

Directions: Science can be used to save the planet. Ideas such as recycling, harnessing natural resources such as wind and water, and cars that run on battery, as opposed to ozone-harmful gas, are all scientific ideas that help protect the Earth's resources and environment. Even though the protection of the planet is a global issue, many times the battle must be fought in individual communities. Different communities contribute in different ways. Which method is the best for helping the planet, and what can we do in our community to help?

Your group of four will research and propose a scientific idea that will help the community protect the Earth's resources and environment. You will need to figure out the cost and implementation of such a program, as well as how to communicate it to the community. Your group will then present to a panel of influential members of the community, discussing why your option is the most realistic and affordable for the community.

You and your group members will take on the following roles:

- **Research Lead:** Responsible for keeping others on task and reviewing the research to make sure it is from legitimate sources.
- **Budget:** Responsible for checking that the budget is realistic and reviewing the math to ensure correctness.
- **Implementation:** Responsible for looking at how the measure would be taken by the city, who would be involved, and the short- and long-term effects.
- **Spokesperson:** Responsible for representing the group at the discussion.

SUGGESTED TIMELINE

DAY				
1 Introduce the project and conduct Lesson: Can You Make a Difference?	**2** Conduct a class discussion about a documentary and have students form groups (see Teacher-Led Discussion Assessment Form).	**3** Have groups begin researching programs communities have used to help the environment (each group member is responsible for finding an example).	**4** Have students continue to research programs that communities have used to help the environment.	**5** Have students continue to research programs that communities have used to help the environment.
6 Conduct group discussions about environmental protection programs (see Group Discussion Assessment Form).	**7** Have groups begin to research and determine the cost and implementation strategies of their project.	**8** Have groups continue to research and determine the cost and implementation strategies of their project.	**9** Have groups continue to research and determine the cost and implementation strategies of their project.	**10** Conduct Lesson: Developing a Proposal (see Handout 3.1).
11 Have groups work on their proposals.	**12** Have groups continue to work on their proposals.	**13** Have groups practice discussing their proposals.	**14** Conduct student-led discussions (see Student-Led Discussion Assessment Form, Product Rubric).	

Can You Make a Difference?

To introduce students to this project, watch a documentary about how the acts people do can help to protect the Earth's resources and environment. Possible documentaries include:

- *An Inconvenient Truth*
- *The Power of Community: How Cuba Survived Peak Oil*
- *Garbage Warrior*
- *No Impact Man*

Teacher-Led Discussion

After watching the documentary, conduct a class discussion about what was done and how beneficial it was to the environment. Assess students' discussion contributions with the Teacher-Led Discussion Assessment Form. Discussion questions may include:

1. Do you think cars should be banned from cities due to the pollution from the exhaust?

2. What are some things that your community is doing to help the environment?

3. What are some things that you recycle? Do you drink a lot of bottled water? What impact do you think that has on the environment?

4. Do you think an individual person can make an impact to help prevent pollution?

5. What can you do to make this world a better place?

6. Which is more important, increasing people's standard of living or protecting the environment?

7. Who do you think is more responsible for helping with pollution, individual people or the government?

8. If you could choose one alternative energy source to develop, which one would you choose?

9. Do you think recycling is an important community service?

10. Who should pay for the costs associated with renewable energy?

11. Should we make the development of renewable energy sources an economic priority?

12. How can we protect the environment and at the same time improve people's standard of living?

13. Does your local government make it easy or hard for citizens to recycle?

14. What should we do to increase the awareness about environmental pollution?

Group Discussions

Within their groups of four, students will take on specific roles. Although all group members will contribute to the project, they are going to be responsible for certain aspects of the project. Each group member needs to take part in researching programs that communities have implemented to help the environment. At the end of the research days, each student is responsible for presenting an example they found. There will be a group discussion about which one to choose and why. Assess students' discussion contributions with the Group Discussion Assessment Form.

Project 3: Group Discussion

Developing a Proposal

Once students have either chosen the idea they want to move forward with or figured out a way to combine ideas, they will need to put together a proposal that will be presented to the panel.

Finding an Authentic Audience

In order to make the proposal more real-world for students, you need to bring in an authentic audience for the students to present to. Some ideas for members of this authentic audience include:

- local officials (mayor, city council),
- members of the city service and utilities,
- principal or other administrators,
- experts on environmental issues (scientists or environmental studies),
- older students,
- waste management officials, or
- parents.

Discussion Day

Students will have 5 minutes to present their proposal to the audience. During this time, students need to answer all of the questions involved in the formation of the proposal.

After the initial presentation, there will be 10 minutes for discussion moderated by the teacher. The discussion can take one of three forms:

- **Discussion in favor:** Supports the proposal given and cites reasons for why.
- **Discussion in opposition:** Does not support the proposal and reasons why or offers better solutions.
- **Question for the speakers:** Has a question concerning the proposal for the speakers, which they have the opportunity to answer (these can also come from the panel).

Once the discussion time has ended, the group has the opportunity to make a final plea to the panel through their spokesperson about why their proposal is worthy of consideration. This might involve refuting things brought up in the discussion, reiterating important points, or adding something to strengthen the argument.

Name: _____ Date: _____

HANDOUT 3.1

Developing a Proposal

Directions: Your group needs to prepare a proposal for your spokesperson to present in the upcoming discussion with the panel of experts. Your proposal will need to include:

- what the plan will involve,
- where the plan has been used before,
- how successful the plan has been in other communities,
- who will be responsible for implementing the program,
- how the plan will involve the community,
- how long the plan will take to implement,
- the estimated cost of implementation,
- the impact the plan will have on the community,
- the short-term benefits of implementing the program, and
- the long-term benefits of implementing the program.

Remember: Your group will have 5 minutes to present your proposal. This will be followed by a discussion about the merits and problems with the proposal. Your group will then have 1 minute to make final comments on the proposal.

© **Prufrock Press Inc.** • *10 Performance-Based Projects for the Science Classroom*

Project 3: Group Discussion

Teacher-Led Discussion

Directions: Put an X or mark where the student is on the scale.

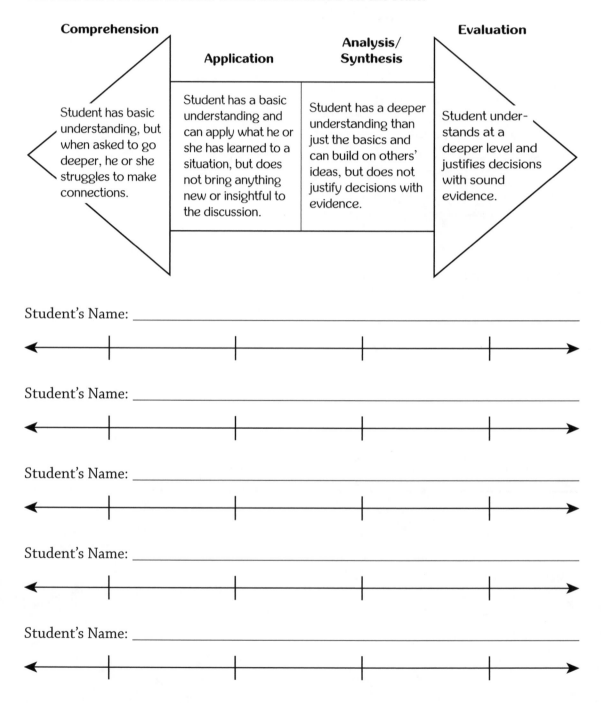

Comprehension

Application

Analysis/ Synthesis

Evaluation

Student has basic understanding, but when asked to go deeper, he or she struggles to make connections.

Student has a basic understanding and can apply what he or she has learned to a situation, but does not bring anything new or insightful to the discussion.

Student has a deeper understanding than just the basics and can build on others' ideas, but does not justify decisions with evidence.

Student understands at a deeper level and justifies decisions with sound evidence.

Student's Name: _____

Student's Name: _____

Student's Name: _____

Student's Name: _____

Student's Name: _____

ASSESSMENT FORM

Group Discussion

Directions: Put an X or mark where the student is on the scale.

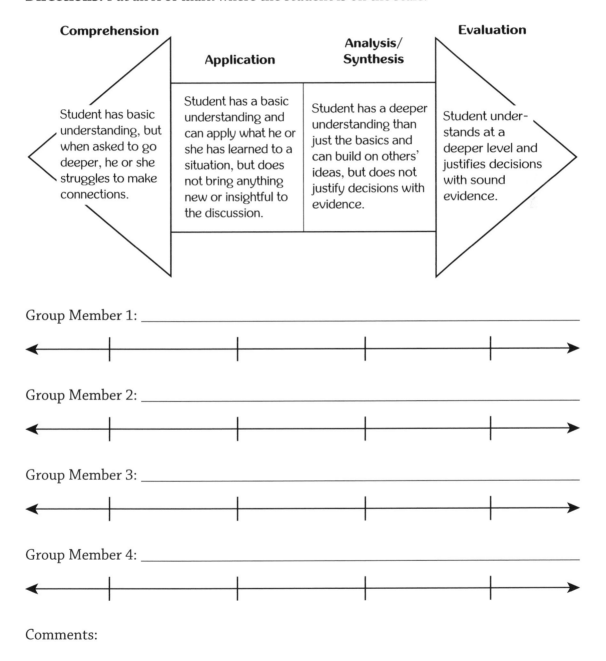

Group Member 1: _____

Group Member 2: _____

Group Member 3: _____

Group Member 4: _____

Comments:

Project 3: Group Discussion

Student-Led Discussion

Directions: Put an X or mark where the student is on the scale.

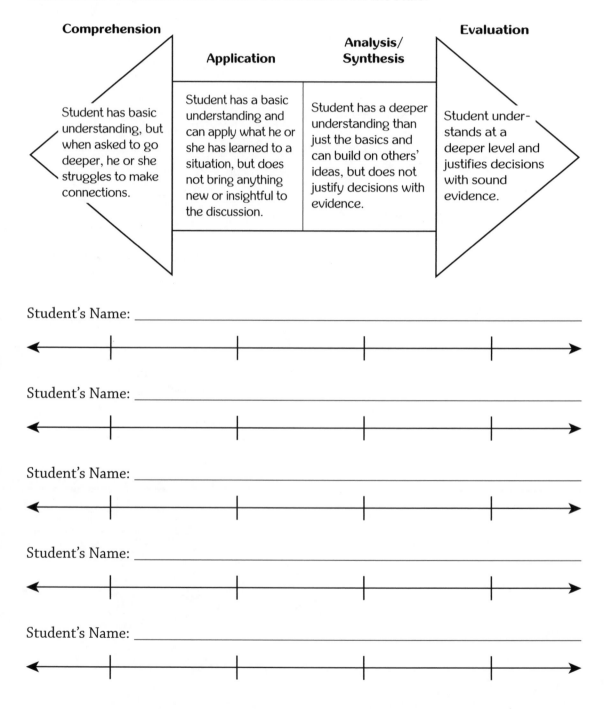

Student's Name: _____

Student's Name: _____

Student's Name: _____

Student's Name: _____

Student's Name: _____

Name: _____ Date: _____

PRODUCT RUBRIC

How Can We Save the Planet?

Overall	Content	Structure	Presentation
Excellent (A)	• Group includes many additional details and examples designed to support the proposal. • Group is able to answer questions posed by audience with confidence. • Group includes many references to research as to the effectiveness of such a program.	• Group clearly covers the requirements of the proposal, going into great detail that shows what it will look like. • Group gives a clear picture as to the cost of the program and how realistic it will be for the community. • Group makes excellent use of the time allotted for the proposal, pacing itself well and balancing information.	• Spokesperson represents the group in a professional manner, showing maturity throughout the proposal. • Spokesperson consistently speaks with confidence in the group's proposal. • Spokesperson is persuasive in the group's arguments, using several techniques to sway the audience as to why their choices are excellent ones.
Good (B–C)	• Group includes additional details and examples but needs more to offer complete support. • Group is able to answer most questions posed by audience but stumbles occasionally. • Group includes a few references to research as to the effectiveness of such a program but needs additional information to be more convincing.	• Group covers the requirements of the proposal in a basic manner but does not go into much detail that shows what it will look like. • Group gives an idea of the cost of the program but not a clear picture of how it will be funded. • Group makes good use of the time allotted for the proposal, although some aspects are rushed.	• Spokesperson most of the time represents the group in a professional manner, but does not maintain this through the entire proposal. • Spokesperson speaks with confidence in group's proposal most of the time but is not consistent throughout. • Spokesperson is persuasive in group's arguments, trying to sway the audience as to why the group's choices are excellent ones with a technique or two.

Product Rubric: How Can We Save the Planet?, *continued*

Overall	Content	Structure	Presentation
Needs Improvement (D–F)	• Group does not include many additional details and examples that would have supported the proposal. • Group is not able to answer most questions posed by audience. • Group does not include many references to research as to the effectiveness of such a program or references they make are incorrect.	• Group does not cover the requirements of the proposal, leaving one to wonder what this will look like. • Group does not give even a basic idea of the cost of the program and/or how it will be funded. • Group does not make good use of the time allotted for the proposal, spending too much time on some aspects and not enough on others.	• Spokesperson does not present the group in a professional manner, showing lack of maturity throughout the proposal. • Spokesperson does not speak with confidence in the group's proposal, looking unsure of him- or herself. • Spokesperson is not persuasive in the group's arguments, not seeming to try and sway the audience as to why the group's choices are excellent ones.

4 Role-Playing

Role-playing is a form of creative oral presentation where a student must inhabit a specific persona and carry out the role from that person's perspective. It allows students to walk a day in the shoes of someone else and helps them to understand different perspectives. A constant struggle with students is to get them to think about anything from another perspective than their own. Giving them opportunities to explore other perspectives will allow them to gain a better understanding of a character, time period, or idea.

What It Looks Like

Role-playing can involve having a person assume the role of a character from a novel to demonstrate how he would react to situations the character had to experience. Or it can involve a mock trial in which a student is given a specific role to play, such as a lawyer, a witness, a defendant, the judge, or even the jury. Although a student is focusing in on her specific role, she is getting an understanding of how a trial works and of the arguments being made.

Dinosaurs on Trial

Dinosaurs lived on our planet millions of years ago, and yet we have never actually seen a dinosaur in the flesh. How do we know they existed?

In this project, students will put the evidence to the test by putting the theory of dinosaurs on trial. Prosecutors will seek to prove that dinosaurs never existed and that fossil records are inaccurate, while the defense will make arguments and present evidence that dinosaurs did exist using the fossil records as their primary evidence. Expert witnesses will be asked to testify for both sides, and a jury will decide which presented better evidence.

Connections to NGSS

- 3-LS4-1

Materials

- Project Outline: Dinosaurs on Trial (student copies)
- Suggested Timeline
- Lesson: The Theory of Dinosaurs
- Lesson: Roles of the Trial
- Handout 4.1: The Prosecution (student copies)
- Handout 4.2: The Defense (student copies)
- Handout 4.3: The Prosecution's Witnesses (student copies)
- Handout 4.4: The Defense's Witnesses (student copies)
- Handout 4.5: The Judge (student copy)
- Handout 4.6: The Jury (student copies)
- Handout 4.7: Witness Preparation Questions (student copies)
- Handout 4.8: Student Reflection (student copies)
- Reflection Rubric (student copies)

PROJECT OUTLINE

Dinosaurs on Trial

Directions: Dinosaurs lived on our planet millions of years ago, and yet we have never actually seen a dinosaur in the flesh. How do we know they existed?

You will put the evidence to the test by putting the theory of dinosaurs on trial, taking on one of the following roles. Prosecutors will seek to prove that dinosaurs never existed and that fossil records are inaccurate, while the defense will make arguments and present evidence that dinosaurs did exist using the fossil records as their primary evidence. Expert witnesses will be asked to testify for both sides, and a jury will decide which presented better evidence.

Project 4: Role-Playing

SUGGESTED TIMELINE

DAY				
1 Introduce the project and conduct Lesson: The Theory of Dinosaurs.	**2** Conduct Lesson: Roles of the Trial.	**3** Assign or have students choose roles for the trial (see Handouts 4.1–4.7).	**4** Have students begin preparing for the trial, reviewing their roles and tasks.	**5** Have students continue preparing for the trial, reviewing their roles and tasks.
6 Have students continue preparing for the trial, reviewing their roles and tasks.	**7** Have students continue preparing for the trial, reviewing their roles and tasks.	**8** Have prosecution and defense interview opposing witnesses and create cross-examination questions.	**9** Have prosecution and defense interview opposing witnesses and create cross-examination questions.	**10** Have students complete trial preparations.
11 Have prosecution and defense make opening statements.	**12** Have prosecution present its case and witnesses.	**13** Have defense present its case and witnesses.	**14** Have prosecution and defense make closing statements; have jury and judge present court's decision.	**15** Have students complete Handout 4.8: Student Reflection (see Product Rubric).

The Theory of Dinosaurs

Introduce the project to students, and conduct a brief discussion. Ask students:

1. *Can someone tell me when dinosaurs existed?* Answers will vary, but students should understand that they lived a long time ago (approximately from 250 million to 65 million years ago).

2. *If they lived so long ago, before such things as video and even photographs, how do we know that they existed at all?* Answers will vary, but students should understand that dinosaur bones and fossils have been found.

3. *How do we know that these are authentic?* Answers will vary, but students should understand that we rely on experts/scientists to verify that the findings are real.

4. *Do all experts and scientists believe in the theory of dinosaurs?* Answers will vary, but ultimately you want them to understand that not all experts/scientists do.

LESSON

Roles of the Trial

Tell students they will each have different roles in the trial and will be responsible for preparing for their roles.

- ◆ **The Prosecution:** Up to three lawyers, one for the opening, one for the examination of witnesses, and one for the closing. These students will need copies of Handout 4.1: The Prosecution, Handout 4.3: The Prosecution's Witnesses, and Handout 4.4: The Defense's Witnesses.

- ◆ **The Defense:** Up to three lawyers, one for the opening, one for the examination of witnesses, and one for the closing. These students will need copies of Handout 4.2: The Defense, Handout 4.3: The Prosecution's Witnesses, and Handout 4.4: The Defense's Witnesses.

- ◆ **The Prosecution's Witnesses:** 10 students (students can play multiple roles if there are not enough). These students will need copies of Handout 4.3: The Prosecution's Witnesses and Handout 4.7: Witness Preparation Questions.

- ◆ **The Defense's Witnesses:** 10 students (students can play multiple roles if there are not enough). These students will need copies of Handout 4.4: The Defense's Witnesses and Handout 4.7: Witness Preparation Questions.

- ◆ **The Judge:** One student who will preside over the case. This student will need Handout 4.5: The Judge. While others are preparing for the trial, this student can research actual court cases.

- ◆ **The Jury:** If you have any students left without a role, they can act as the jury. These students will need Handout 4.6: The Jury. While the others are preparing for the trial, the members of the jury can research actual court cases.

Trial Schedule

1. **Opening Statement:** The prosecutor goes first, followed by the defense attorney. Both sides will explain to the judge and jury briefly what they wish to prove and how that will be done.

2. **Presentation of the State's Case:** The burden of proving an accused person committed a crime is always on the state. A defendant is assumed innocent until proven guilty. The prosecutor will provide all of the state's evidence, including facts, witnesses, and physical evidence.

3. **Presentation of the Defense's Case:** The defense attorney for the accused person has an opportunity to show why his or her client is either innocent or justified in committing the crime. Like the prosecutor before him or her, the defense attorney must present evidence to make his or her case stronger.

4. **Closing Arguments:** Once both sides are finished presenting their cases, the prosecutor, and then the defense attorney, will give their final statements to the jury. These remarks focus on the strengths (prosecutor) or weaknesses (defense) of the state's case.

5. **Jury Deliberations:** Members of the jury are placed in a private conference room and ordered to reach a decision or verdict. It is arrived at after careful discussion of the facts of the case, followed by a vote as to whether the person is guilty or not guilty.

6. **Presenting the Verdict:** The foreman (head juror) of the court reads the jury's decision. A "not guilty" verdict means the defense was the most convincing. A "guilty" verdict means the prosecution was more persuasive.

HANDOUT 4.1

The Prosecution

Directions: The prosecution is responsible for bringing charges against the accused.

Prosecution Schedule

1. **The prosecution begins with its opening statement.** This is a short statement as to why the accused should be found guilty of the crime they are accused. The defense follows with its own opening statement about why the accused is innocent.

2. **The prosecution presents its case.** Evidence is provided through witness testimony in order to prove the defendant's guilt. The defense lawyer is allowed to cross-examine any witnesses the prosecution presents, in order to find fault in their testimony. If at any time the defense asks a witness a question that the prosecution thinks is unfair or inappropriate, the prosecution can object, which means the judge will either sustain and stop the questioning or overrule and let the questioning continue.

3. **The defense presents its case.** Evidence is provided through witness testimony, and the prosecution is allowed to cross-examine.

4. **The prosecution presents its closing argument.** Once each side has presented its case, the prosecution gives its closing argument first. The closing argument is the summary of why the defendant should be found guilty. The defense then presents its closing argument.

5. **The verdict is presented.** Then it is up to the judge or jury to decide whether the defendant is innocent or not.

Prosecution Strategies

♦ Establish the credibility of your expert witnesses. You should prepare the questions you are going to ask them at trial. You will want to come up with the best questions to make your case. You and the witness should come up with the answers together. This is known as preparing the witness. Because there are no eyewitnesses to the existence of dinosaurs, you will be relying on expert witnesses.

♦ Present scientific evidence that shows that dinosaurs may not have existed.

Handout 4.1: The Prosecution, *continued*

- ◆ Develop possible counterarguments that might be presented by the other side and determine ways to refute them.
- ◆ Be sure your witnesses research their characters and add any detail or facts that they find. They can also locate evidence that can be presented at the trial.
- ◆ Review the defense's witnesses. Because you are permitted to cross-examine each witness, you will want to jot down possible questions you would ask each of these witnesses in order to find flaws in their testimony.

Name: _____ Date: _____

HANDOUT 4.2

The Defense

Directions: The defense is responsible for defending the accused against the allegations of the prosecution.

Defense Schedule

1. After the prosecution gives its opening statement, the defense gives one of its own, giving its reasons why the charges brought against the accused are false.

2. The prosecution then presents its evidence, calling witnesses to the stand to back up their charges. The defense has the opportunity to cross-examine these witnesses in order to ask questions and find fault with their testimony. At any time during the prosecution's questioning, if the defense feels there has been an improper or inappropriate question, it may object. The judge will either overrule and allow the questioning to continue, or he or she will sustain and prevent the question from being asked.

3. Next, the defense calls its own witnesses to the stand. These witnesses are to disprove the allegations of the prosecution. The prosecution is allowed to cross-examine as well.

4. Once both sides have presented, each side gives its closing argument, the prosecution going first. In the defense's closing argument, it will want to sum up the weaknesses in the case that the prosecution presented and try to put in the jury's mind a shadow of doubt about its client's guilt.

Defense Strategies

- Establish the credibility of your expert witnesses. You should prepare the questions you are going to ask them at trial. You will want to come up with the best questions to make your case. You and the witness should come up with the answers together. This is known as preparing the witness. Because there are no eyewitnesses to the existence of dinosaurs, you will be relying on expert witnesses.
- Present scientific evidence as to the existence of dinosaurs.
- Develop possible counterarguments that might be presented by the other side and determine ways to refute them.

Handout 4.2: The Defense, *continued*

- Be sure your witnesses research their characters and add any detail or facts that they find. They can also locate evidence that can be presented at the trial.
- Review the prosecution's witnesses. Because you are permitted to cross-examine each witness, you will want to jot down possible questions you would ask each of these witnesses in order to find flaws in their testimony.

Project 4: Role-Playing

HANDOUT 4.3

The Prosecution's Witness List

1. **Sir Richard Owen, British Museum Natural History Department:** He hypothesized the existence of dinosaurs in the 1800s before any dinosaur fossils had ever been found. It wasn't until 12 years later that the first supposed dinosaur fossils in the form of teeth were found.

2. **Othniel Marsh, Peabody Museum of Natural History:** He claimed to have discovered more than 500 ancient species, including 80 dinosaurs. However, only 32 of these are considered valid. Most of his work involved reconstructions rather than the discovery of a complete set of bones. In fact, no complete dinosaur skeleton has ever been found, meaning all dinosaurs are reconstructions of what they might have looked like.

3. **David Wozney, writer of "Dinosaurs: Science or Science Fiction":** He makes the argument that the business of dinosaur bones is a profitable one. T. rex bones have fetched as much as $12 million. Museums will pay a lot of money for what they believe to be dinosaur bones, so it would be possible for someone to sell bones and let people's imaginations and interpretations take over.

4. **Robbin Koefoed, author of "The Dinosaurs Never Existed":** He will testify that only around 2,100 dinosaur bones have been discovered worldwide, none of which have formed a complete skeleton. If thousands of dinosaurs had really roamed the Earth, there would be millions of dinosaur bones to find.

5. **Alan Feduccia, Paleontology Professor from the University of North Carolina:** He will talk about the fake fossil factory where bones are created out of plaster and other materials in Northeast China, where many dinosaur findings were made.

6. **Margaret Helder, author of *Completing the Picture, A Handbook on Museum and Interpretive Centers Dealing with Fossils*:** She argues that the dating of fossils and rocks is inaccurate, and the measurements that dating machines make may not tell us much about the actual age of the rock. There is a chance of mistakes because it is not the fossils that are dated but the rocks they are found around. Fossils could have been buried deep to make them appear older than they are.

Handout 4.3: The Prosecution's Witness List, *continued*

7. **Storrs L. Olson, Curator of Birds at the National Museum of Natural History:** He will testify that a 1999 fossil find, purported to be the missing link between birds and dinosaurs, named the Archaeoraptor by *National Geographic*, was actually a hoax. The fossil was a composite of several other fossils and was a forgery meant to convince people that dinosaurs had evolved into birds. It was discovered that the left and right feet mirrored each other perfectly, and no connection could be seen between the tail and the body.

8. **Christopher Bronk Ramsey, Geochronologist at the University of Oxford:** He can testify to the unreliability of carbon-14 date testing. Some examples of abnormal carbon-14 results include testing of recently harvested, live mollusk shells from the Hawaiian coast that showed that they had died 2,000 years ago and snail shells just killed in Nevada, dated in at 27,000 years old. A freshly killed seal at McMurdo Sound, Antarctica, yielded a death age of 1,300 years ago. A petrified miner's hat and wooden fence posts were unearthed from an abandoned 19th-century gold hunter's town in Australia's outback. Results from radiocarbon dating said that they were 6,000 years old. These cause archaeologists to question their earlier conclusions about archaeological sites.

9. An additional witness the group has found from research.

10. An additional witness the group has found from research.

HANDOUT 4.4

The Defense's Witness List

1. **Joseph Leidy, American Paleontologist:** He discovered the Hadrosaurus in 1858. This was the first near-complete dinosaur fossil ever to be excavated in the United States. Hadrosaurus lends it moniker to a huge family of duck-billed dinosaurs—the hadrosaurs—but experts still debate whether the original "type fossil" merits its genus designation.

2. **Edwin Colbert, Curator of the National History Museum in New York:** He unearthed a dozen Coelophysis skeletons at Ghost Ranch, NM, in 1947, which showed that at least some genera of small theropods traveled in vast herds—and that large populations of dinosaurs, meat-eaters and plant-eaters alike, were regularly drowned by flash floods.

3. **Willard Libby, Physical Chemist:** He developed the method of carbon dating. Carbon dating is a variety of radioactive dating, which can be used only on matter that was once living, taking in carbon dioxide from the air for photosynthesis. The radioactive carbon-14 combines with oxygen to form carbon dioxide. The carbon-14 forms at a rate that appears to be constant, so by measuring the radioactive emissions from once-living matter and comparing, time elapsed can be measured.

4. **Dong Zhiming, Chinese Paleontologist:** He discovered the Dashanpu Formation in China's Sichuan province, which has yielded a huge number of remains, dating to the middle Jurassic period, about 170 to 160 million years ago. He spearheaded paleontological research in Northwest China and the Gobi Desert in Mongolia and established the existence of the homalocephale.

5. **Dr. Jose Luis Carballido, Argentina's Museum of Palaeontology:** He discovered in the desert near La Flecha what is believed to be the largest dinosaur. Based on the size of the thighbones, which are taller than an average man, the dinosaur would have been 130 feet long and 65 feet tall. Paleontologists have retrieved some 150 bones said to come from seven individuals, all in remarkable condition.

6. **David Fastovsky, University of Rhode Island:** He discovered a nest in 2011 containing the fossilized remains of 15 juvenile Protoceratops andrewsi dinosaurs. Believed to be a 70-million-year-old nest, the discovery also shows that the

Handout 4.4: The Defense's Witness List, *continued*

young dinosaurs remained in the nest throughout the early stages of postnatal development and were cared for by their parents.

7. **Spencer Lucas, Chief Curator of the New Mexico Museum of Natural History and Science:** He is an expert on trace fossils. Trace fossils are not parts of an animal or impressions of it, but rather evidence of an animal's presence in a given location. Trace fossils include preserved footprints, trails, animal holes, and even feces. By comparing these clues with what is known about modern animals, scientists can learn how prehistoric animals may have lived, what they ate, and how they behaved. For instance, dinosaur tracks can be studied to learn how fast dinosaurs ran.

8. **Professor Gabriela Mángano, University of Saskatchewan:** She discovered a huge number of fossilized trilobite tracks in rocks from the Appalachian Mountains known as mold fossils. Some fossils that form in sedimentary rock are mold fossils. A mold is a visible shape that was left after an animal or plant was buried in sediment and then decayed away. The fossils found in the Appalachian Mountains revealed trilobites moved closer to the land during the Cambrian explosion some 540 million years ago.

9. An additional witness the group has found from research.

10. An additional witness the group has found from research.

HANDOUT 4.5

The Judge

Directions: The judge is the key officer of the court. He or she controls the proceedings of the case, and his or her principal job is to administer the law. A judge is essentially the boss of the courtroom; however, his or her opinion in the case is unbiased. In other words, judges do not pick sides.

♦ If the courtroom is becoming noisy or out of hand, the judge may call for order in the court. If someone misbehaves in the courtroom or fails to follow a judge's orders, that person may be cited in contempt of court.

♦ While hearing a case, the lawyer who is not questioning the witness may disagree with a question being asked. This is known as objecting. A lawyer objects because he or she believes the question is either unfair or improper. The judge has two options when a lawyer objects: He or she can either overrule, which means allow the questioning to continue as it has been, or sustain, which means the lawyer cannot continue to ask the question.

Your job in this activity is one of the most important. You control the pace of the court case and must keep things moving along. The case should proceed in the following order upon your directions.

1. **"Will the prosecution give their opening statement?"** The prosecution always goes first. This starts the case off and sets the tone for what the prosecution is going to try and prove.

2. **"Will the defense present their opening statement?"** This is the defense's response to the accusations of the prosecution.

3. This sequence will repeat itself through all of the prosecution's witnesses:
   a. **"Will the prosecution call their first/next witness?"** The prosecution will call 10 witnesses to the stand to present their case.
   b. **"Would the defense like to cross-examine the witness?"** The defense can cross-examine any witness the prosecution uses, trying to find fault with their testimony.
   c. **"The witness is excused."** The judge says this every time the lawyers are finished with a witness.

Handout 4.5: The Judge, *continued*

4. This sequence will repeat itself through all of the defense's witnesses:
   a. **"Will the defense call their first/next witness?"** The defense will also call 10 witnesses to the stand and ask each one of them no more than three questions.
   b. **"Would the prosecution like to cross-examine the witness?"** The prosecution can cross-examine any witness the defense uses, but can ask no more than two questions.
   c. **"The witness is excused."** The judge says this every time the lawyers are finished with a witness.

5. The court takes a 5-minute recess for the lawyers to prepare their closing.

6. The prosecution gives its closing argument. The prosecution will sum up their case and why the accused should be found guilty.

7. The defense gives its closing argument. The defense will sum up the weaknesses in the prosecution's case and why the accused should be found innocent.

8. The jury will now deliberate. This is when the jury will make their decision and vote on the verdict. If there is a jury, they will be excused to deliberate on the verdict.

9. **"Has the jury reached a verdict?"** This is when the foreman (head juror) will read the jury's verdict.

Project 4: Role-Playing

HANDOUT 4.6

The Jury

Directions: As members of the jury, you will need to select a foreman (head juror) who is in charge of deliberation as well as reading the final verdict. The foreman should read and discuss the following information with the other jurors.

A jury functions as the center of the justice system. They are the peers of the accused—in other words, regular people just like them, not involved in the everyday life of the court system. Jurors must make the tough decision of whether the evidence against the accused is strong enough to convict (find them guilty) or to acquit (find them innocent). This decision is based on the review of the evidence that has been presented, not on opinion. If the evidence leads the jurors to believe that the accused is guilty, then they should vote as thus. If, however, there is a shadow of doubt—in other words, the evidence is not strong enough to prove guilt—then they must vote "not guilty."

Jurors should be unbiased, or have no prior judgment on the case before they enter the courtroom. Juries are selected from a pool of potential jurors who are asked questions by the prosecution and defense attorneys to see whether the person will make a good jury member for their case. The lawyers are allowed to dismiss only a certain amount of jurors. Once 12 people have been selected, these 12 may not discuss the case with anyone else nor speak directly to the court during the trial. They are only to listen in order to make a decision based on what they have heard.

After the closing arguments of the lawyers, the jury then deliberates, or reviews the case, behind closed doors away from the lawyers, witnesses, and judge. They are placed in a private conference room and must reach either a verdict of "guilty" or "not guilty." They discuss the case among themselves to try to reach a unanimous decision. If they cannot all agree on the verdict, this is known as a hung jury and the accused can go free.

After their decision has been made, the jury once again enters the courtroom and the foreman reads the verdict to the court. If the jury finds the defendant guilty, they must then return to their chambers in order to decide a sentence for the accused. They must determine a punishment that fits the crime within the law.

As the jury, your main job is to listen to the case presented and, based solely on the evidence, make a decision. Do not play favorites to your friends or allow prior beliefs to make your decision. Which side presented themselves the best?

During the preparation part of the trial, each jury member is responsible for reading about a famous trial and pretending you are a juror in it. After reading all of the evidence and information about the case, choose which verdict you would choose and why you would. You will write about this decision in a one-page synopsis describing the case, your decision, and what convinced you.

Name: _____ Date: _____

HANDOUT 4.7

Witness Preparation Questions

Directions: Write at least five questions your lawyers are going to ask you during the trial and how you plan to respond to them.

1.

2.

3.

4.

5.

HANDOUT 4.8

Student Reflection

Directions: Answer the following reflection questions with lots of detail to support your knowledge and opinions.

1. What did you learn about fossils during the trial?

2. How do fossils provide evidence of the organisms and the environments in which dinosaurs lived?

3. How important is the study of fossils to understanding organisms and environments that existed a long time ago—before there was even written history?

Name: _____ Date: _____

REFLECTION RUBRIC

Dinosaurs on Trial

A	• **Part I:** Student includes that they understand that various types of fossils are used to determine what life was like before recorded history and that it is not always an exact science. He or she shows a balance of information from the two perspectives. • **Part 2:** Student mentions various types of fossils including, but not limited to, trace, mold, and true fossil forms. He or she also includes several specific examples of discovered fossils that were cited in the trial and what was learned from them. • **Part 3**: Student explains the importance of fossils and how they let scientists and historians put together missing information, much like putting together a puzzle that has some missing pieces.
B	Same as above except several examples are not detailed enough or only a few are provided for all three parts.
C	Same as above except several examples are very general or the student only provides one example to make his or her point(s) for all three parts.
D	Reflection addresses two of the parts but either does not include a third or the response given is incorrect for the third and includes false information.
F	Reflection has two or more responses that are simply incorrect or include false information.

Project 4: Role-Playing

5 Interview

Students often imagine teachers as the experts of their disciplines. If you are a language arts teacher, you are expected to be able to spell every single word in the English language correctly or to have read every book in the library. If you are a math teacher, you should know how to solve any math problem or know all of the mathematical principles that govern the discipline.

We as teachers know the truth: There are times when we simply do not know the answer, or we are teaching a topic we are not comfortable with. Having students interview an expert on a topic is a good learning tool that provides a real-world connection. Not only that, unlike using a book or the Internet to find an answer, the students can ask exactly what it is they want to know and receive an instant answer. There is no inferring or reading between the lines. It is a direct way to get content and insight about a topic.

What It Looks Like

Interviews can be done in a couple of ways. One way is for the student herself to locate an expert in a topic she wants to know more about and conduct an individual interview. The interview is tailored to this student's needs and she gains valuable information from the source.

A second way to conduct an interview is for the teacher to bring in an expert or panel of experts for the students to question. There does need to be a format to this process. You do not want to just turn students loose to ask any questions that come to mind. Students might ask off-topic questions or even inappropriate ones, and time that could have been spent getting valuable insight from the speaker is wasted. Bringing in an expert can take the learning to a deeper, more meaningful level.

You Can Make a Living Out of Doing Science?

In this project, students will each select and research a career in the field of science. As part of their research, they must locate someone who is currently involved in this career and interview him or her about the profession. They will then write a paper about their findings.

Connections to NGSS

- 3-LS3-1
- 3-LS4-1
- 3-ESS2-2
- 4-PS4-2
- 4-LS1-2
- 4-ESS1-1
- 5-PS1-1
- 5-PS1-4
- 5-ESS1-1

Note. Standards will vary based upon the career each student studies.

Materials

- Project Outline: You Can Make a Living Doing Science? (student copies)
- Suggested Timeline
- Handout 5.1: How to Conduct an Interview (student copies)
- Handout 5.2: Revising Your Draft (student copies)
- Product Rubric (student copies)

Name: _____ Date: _____

You Can Make a Living Doing Science?

Directions: Believe it or not, there are several careers that involve applying the skills of science. Some of these would be engineers, doctors, paleontologists, meteorologists, marine biologists, and many more.

You will research a career in the field of science (see http://www.sciencebuddies.org/science-engineering-careers for ideas). As part of this research, you must locate someone who is currently involved in this career and interview him or her about the work the profession requires. You will then write a paper about the career.

There should be four sections to your paper:

- Introduction
  ◊ What is the career you chose to research?
  ◊ What about it interests you?
  ◊ How strong do you consider yourself in science or your interest in science?

- Career opportunities
  ◊ What exactly does someone do in this career?
  ◊ What are the opportunities in this line of work?
  ◊ Are jobs plentiful, or is there a hierarchy in the job field that you have to work your way up?
  ◊ Are there many people doing this job, or are there only a few select experts?
  ◊ How much science is used in this job and for what purposes?

- Training for the profession
  ◊ Is there special training or school to be in this profession? What does this encompass?
  ◊ What sort of science background would someone need in order to be in this profession?
  ◊ How important would it be in this profession to continue learning about science in order to keep up with changes and innovations? Where does that learning occur?

- Conclusion
  ◊ Is this career what you expected it would be?
  ◊ Now that you have researched it, are you interested in pursuing this career?
  ◊ Do you think pursuing this career will be a difficult or easy task, and why?

SUGGESTED TIMELINE

DAY				
1 Introduce the project and have students begin research-ing careers.	**2** Have students select a career and continue researching it.	**3** Distribute Handout 5.1: How to Conduct an Interview and review it with students.	**4** Have students continue researching their career, as well as experts in the field.	**5** Have students continue researching their career, as well as experts in the field.
6 Have students select and con-tact interview subjects.	**7** Students need to begin the rough draft of their career paper and/or interview their subject.	**8** Students need to continue the rough draft of their career paper and/or interview their subject.	**9** Students need to continue the rough draft of their career paper and/or interview their subject.	**10** Students need to continue the rough draft of their career paper and/or interview their subject.
11 Students need to complete the rough draft of their career paper and the interview of their subject.	**12** Distribute Handout 5.2: Revising Your Draft and review it with students.	**13** Students need to begin the final draft of their career paper.	**14** Students need to continue the final draft of their career paper.	**15** Students need to continue the final draft of their career paper.
16 Students need to fin-ish the final draft of their career paper (see Product Rubric).				

Name: _____ Date: _____

HANDOUT 5.1

How to Conduct an Interview

Directions: As part of this project, you will interview a mentor, who will offer advice about your chosen career. The following steps will help you prepare and conduct your interview.

1. Know your stuff. The best way to generate interview questions is to know as much as you can. Create a list of 15 specific questions that can be answered with more than "yes" or "no." You want to get your interviewee talking.

2. Be polite when you contact your interviewee, and ask when a good time would be to do the interview. An in-person interview is ideal, but a phone interview is acceptable.

3. Come prepared with a pen or pencil, a notebook, a recording device, and your questions. Practice your questions in advance. If you plan to record your interview, be sure to ask permission.

4. Be professional:
   ◇ Arrive (or call) on time.
   ◇ Be polite and look your interviewee in the eye.
   ◇ Listen carefully; ask follow-up questions and for more information about things you don't understand.
   ◇ Act naturally. Although it is an interview, it should still feel like a conversation.

5. Even if you are recording, take notes. Don't try to write every word. Just take down the important things. After the interview, expand your notes with what you remember and by conducting more research. Highlight what you think are the most important points.

Note. Adapted from "How to Conduct a Journalistic Interview" by Scholastic News Kids Press Corps, n.d., retrieved from http://www.scholastic.com/teachers/article/how-conduct-journalistic-interview.

Project 5: Interview

Name: _____ Date: _____

Revising Your Draft

Directions: Edit your paper for correct grammar, spelling, sentence structure, and content, using the following tips.

1. **First Round of Editing:** Using the project outline, make sure everything is discussed and answered in detail. Read your paper, pretending you know nothing about your topic and this paper is teaching you everything you need to know about it.

2. **Second Round of Editing:** Using spell check is not always enough. You need to go through the paper and make sure things are spelled correctly and that the correct forms of words are used.

3. **Third Round of Editing:** During this round, you will want to find a place where you can read the paper out loud. This is a good way to check that your sentence structure is clear and that what you are writing makes sense. If you have trouble saying a sentence out loud, chances are a person reading it will also struggle. Fix these awkward sentences so that your paper makes sense and flows.

4. **Final Round of Editing:** Use the rubric as a checklist to make sure you have met all of the requirements of the research paper and that it is of the quality level you want it to be. If there are sections that seem to need improvement, what can be changed to get them into the excellent range?

Name: _____ Date: _____

PRODUCT RUBRIC

You Can Make a Living Doing Science?

Career: _____

Overall	Content	Paper	Research
Excellent (A)	◆ Paper follows the outline clearly, allowing the reader to know what is being discussed at any given time. ◆ Student gives plenty of examples to back up statements made in the paper. ◆ Student provides much detail, explaining concepts and ideas so that the reader can gain a full understanding of what is being talked about.	◆ Paper has little to no spelling/grammatical errors. ◆ Paper is typed in the correct format. ◆ Paper uses a sentence structure that makes the paragraphs flow and easy to read.	◆ Research is consistently put into student's own words, paraphrasing the information. ◆ Student uses specific facts and data where necessary, giving the reader a clear picture of the career. ◆ Student uses several quotes from the interview to convey information and make points.
Good (B–C)	◆ Paper follows the outline, but doesn't always allow the reader to know what is being discussed at any given time. ◆ Student gives examples to back up statements made in the paper in most places but not consistently. ◆ Student provides detail, explaining concepts and ideas so that the reader can gain an understanding of what is being talked about but could be clearer.	◆ Paper has the occasional spelling/grammatical errors, making more than a handful of mistakes. ◆ Paper is typed but not always in the correct format. ◆ Paper mostly uses a sentence structure that makes the paragraphs flow and easy to read, but has the occasional awkward sentence that causes confusion.	◆ Research is put into student's own words, paraphrasing the information, but occasionally using terms and phrases not his or her own. ◆ Student uses facts and data but may not be very specific or not in every place it is needed. ◆ Student uses a couple of quotes from the interview to convey information and make points but could use more.

© **Prufrock Press Inc.** • *10 Performance-Based Projects for the Science Classroom*

This page may be photocopied or reproduced with permission for single classroom use only.

81

Product Rubric: You Can Make a Living Doing Science?, *continued*

Overall	Content	Paper	Research
Needs Improvement (D–F)	• Paper does not follow the outline, causing the reader confusion about what is being discussed at any given time because parts are left out. • Student provides little to no examples to back up statements made in the paper. • Student does not provide much detail, leaving the reader confused about what is being talked about.	• Paper has many spelling/grammatical errors, making it difficult to read the paper at times. • Paper is typed in a sloppy manner, making it difficult to read. • Paper has a sloppy sentence structure that makes the paragraphs difficult to follow and unclear.	• Research is many times not put into the student's own words and uses terms and phrases not his or her own. • Student does not use facts and data where necessary, leaving the reader with more questions than answers. • Student uses little to no quotes from the interview to convey information and make points.

6 Exhibition

An exhibition is just as it states: an exhibit of what the students have learned. An audience usually views the exhibition, whether it is made up of other students in the class, other classes from the school, parents, or outside audience members. The tricky thing about an exhibition is that the students cannot explain themselves orally; they must let the work explain itself. The analogy I often use with students when demonstrating an exhibition is the telling of a joke: "Two guys walk into a bar. The third one ducks." Nearly every time I tell this joke, I get puzzled looks and furrowed brows. I always feel a need to explain the joke: "You see, the bar in this case is not an establishment where one purchases alcohol. The bar is an actual metal bar that the people physically walk into . . ."

It's hilarious, right? Wrong. Because I have to explain the joke, it is not funny (no matter how much I think it is). Exhibitions are the exact same way. If you have to verbally explain the exhibit, the exhibit is not accomplishing what it is supposed to. When you go to an art exhibition, the artist is not there to explain what she did and why she did it. The piece has to stand on its own merits.

What It Looks Like

How a student approaches an exhibition is very different from other PBAs. Let us say for the sake of argument that a student creates a trifold

83

as a product. If the student were using an oral presentation as this performance assessment, he might have a few meaningful visuals such as photos or graphs to enhance his explanation. He would not write out everything he plans to say on the board. Otherwise, he will feel compelled to read it verbatim and give a very stiff oral presentation. In an exhibition, the explanation would need to be written out because there is no one there to orally explain it.

An exhibition can come in many forms. A few common ones include:
- trifold,
- poster,
- PowerPoint presentation,
- short story/poem,
- video,
- piece of artwork or a craft, or
- photography series.

No matter which form a student chooses, first and foremost it must inform the audience and allow it to learn from the exhibition.

City of the Future

In this project, students will work in groups to design a city 25 years in the future that is powered by a more responsible energy. This will involve researching renewable sources of energy and understanding how energy gets converted from one form to another. They will create a model of their city that shows how it will be powered.

Connections to NGSS

- 4-PS3-4
- 4-ESS3-1

Materials

- Project Outline: City of the Future (student copies)
- Suggested Timeline
- Lesson: What Makes a City a City?

- Lesson: Converting Energy
- Handout 6.1: Designing Your City (student copies)
- Handout 6.2: Creating Your City Plan and Model (student copies)
- Product Rubric (student copies)

PROJECT OUTLINE

City of the Future

When *Back to the Future II* released in 1989, the filmmakers predicted a future 25 years later where there would be flying cars, hovering skateboards, self-tying shoes, and devices that could transform trash into fuel. Unfortunately for us, they were way off, but here is your chance to create the city of the future, in which your team will figure out a way to power it using responsible energy. This will involve researching renewable sources of energy and understanding how energy gets converted from one form to another. Your group will create a model of your city that shows how it will be powered.

Members of your group will take on the following roles:

- **Head Researcher:** Responsible for making sure various types of renewable energy are researched and that the team has the information needed in order to make a well-informed decision.
- **City Planner:** Responsible for the overall design of the city and making sure the team produces a quality plan.
- **Engineer:** Responsible for the construction of the model and making sure it matches the plan and fulfills the requirements of the project.

SUGGESTED TIMELINE

DAY				
1 Introduce the project and conduct Lesson: What Makes a City a City?	**2** Conduct Lesson: Converting Energy.	**3** Have students form groups and begin researching different types of renewable energy.	**4** Have students form groups and continue researching different types of renewable energy.	**5** Have groups decide how they want to power their city (see Handout 6.1).
6 Have groups begin creating their city plan (see Handout 6.2).	**7** Have groups continue creating their city plan.	**8** Have groups continue creating their city plan.	**9** Have groups continue creating their city plan.	**10** Have groups finish creating their city plan, deciding what materials are going to be used to construct their model.
11 Have groups begin model construction.	**12** Have groups continue model construction.	**13** Have groups continue model construction.	**14** Have groups continue model construction.	**15** Evaluate city plans and models (see Product Rubric).

What Makes a City a City?

Ask students: *What makes a city a city?* Possible answers include schools, police, fire departments, parks, stores, restaurants, hospitals, libraries, etc. Further discussion questions include:

+ What ensures the safety of the citizens of the city?
+ What ensures the betterment of the citizens of the city?
+ What ensures the growth of the city?
+ What allows the city to function?
+ What would happen to the city if it didn't have any energy?
+ How does a city provide energy to its citizens?

Ask: *Do you know what an infrastructure is?* Infrastructure is the basic physical and organizational structures and facilities (e.g., buildings, roads, and power supplies) needed for the operation of a city. These are what the National Infrastructure Protection Plan (U.S. Department of Homeland Security, 2015) deemed critical infrastructure for a city:

+ commercial facilities,
+ communications,
+ manufacturing,
+ dams,
+ defense industrial base,
+ emergency services,
+ energy,
+ financial services,
+ food and agriculture,
+ government facilities,
+ healthcare and public health,
+ information technology,
+ transportation systems, and
+ water and wastewater systems.

Ask: *Why are these necessary for a city to run?* (Hint: If you take them away, what would happen to the city?) *Which of these do you think is the most important?* There might be some debate on this question, but ultimately you will want to direct students to the idea of energy (one way to convince them is to have them imagine their lives without any electricity).

Converting Energy

Tell students that the simplest example of converting energy is photosynthesis, which involves taking the light from the sun and turning it into food for plants. Photosynthesis takes place in the leaves of plants. The leaves are made up of very small cells inside of which are tiny structures called *chloroplasts*. Each chloroplast contains a green chemical called *chlorophyll* which gives leaves their green color. They are converting the energy of the sun into food for themselves.

Other examples of converting energy include:

- chemical energy from the burning of coal, oil, and natural gas;
- solar panels converting the sun;
- wind turbines using the friction provided by the winds;
- nuclear energy using fusion and fission;
- dams and tidal power taking the energy from moving water;
- steam engines; and
- geothermal energy taking the heat that emits naturally from the planet and converting it.

HANDOUT 6.1

Designing Your City

Directions: Review the following things to consider and design steps as you begin planning your city.

Things to Consider

1. What does your city absolutely need?

2. What would be nice for your city but is not necessary?

3. How many of the 14 necessary infrastructures do you have?

4. What will be the major form of transportation in your city, and what sort of environmental issues might this cause?

5. Where will you place the buildings in your town?

6. What sort of jobs will be available in the city?

7. What types of resources are available to your city?

8. Is the city self-sufficient or will people need to go other places to find things (i.e., jobs, stores, schools, food, etc.)?

9. Have you given the city room to grow and develop?

10. Have you made it able to function as a 21st-century city?

Name: _____ Date: _____

Handout 6.1: Designing Your City, *continued*

Steps to Designing Your City

1. Figure out the terrain. Are you near the ocean, lots of farming land, flat spaces for housing, etc.?

2. Decide what is most important to your city. You will probably want to centralize it by placing this in the center of your city. You will build your city off of this in tangents.

3. Decide what infrastructure you will need in order to function as a city.

4. Determine how you will both physically and technologically connect sections of your city.

5. Place buildings strategically throughout the city. In other words, you do not want two elementary schools on one side of town and none on the other.

6. Make sure there is a balance amongst your city. If you have a high population, you will need more police or fire personnel than if you have a smaller population.

Name: _____ Date: _____

Creating Your City Plan and Model

Creating Your Plan

1. Make it look professional. Use graph paper and proper drawing tools (i.e., ruler, compass, etc.). Use a pencil for the initial drawing and then go over with pen. Make the design large enough for others to tell what it is.

2. Label the plan, writing clearly in print. Estimate distances (i.e., how many miles across). Be creative—name your parks, your schools, and your roads.

3. Be realistic—make sure the city is functional. Don't forget that your main goal is to find a way to power your city using a renewable power source and the plan should center around that.

Creating Your Model

Your model needs to:
* be 3-D,
* be clearly labeled,
* have elements created to scale,
* show how energy will be transformed from one mode to another and how this will power the entire city,
* be of high quality and pleasing to the eye,
* match the design you created for your city, and
* be portable.

You could represent certain aspects with the following materials:
* **Trees:** Twigs and sticks with cotton balls (painted green), dried flowers or weeds, or sponges with food coloring
* **People:** Sticks, toothpicks, pipe cleaners, or Lego figures
* **Glass:** Clear plastic dividers, sleeves, sheets, or clear plastic wrap
* **Roads:** Black paper cut to size with drawn-on lane markers
* **Sidewalks:** Gray paper cut to size
* **Water:** Blue paper cut to size
* **Sand/beach:** Sandpaper or brown sugar
* **Grass:** Green paper or a "grass material" or green felt or fabric

Name: _____ Date: _____

PRODUCT RUBRIC

City of the Future

Overall	Research	Plan	Model
Excellent (A)	◆ Students obtain and combine detailed information to show how energy and fuels are derived from natural resources and how they affect the environment. ◆ Students clearly apply scientific ideas to design, test, and refine a device to power their city. ◆ Model and plan show evidence of thorough research and planning.	◆ Plan clearly demonstrates how energy will be distributed throughout the city and the benefits of the choice of power. ◆ Plan looks professional and realistic and is clearly labeled. ◆ Plan gives a clear idea of how the city will be able to expand and grow.	◆ Model provides a clear idea of how the city will be laid out and how the elements will work together. ◆ Model closely represents how energy will be distributed throughout the city and benefits of the choice of power. ◆ Model is professional looking, bringing the city to life.
Good (B–C)	◆ Students obtain and combine information to show that energy and fuels are derived from natural resources and how they affect the environment, but could use more detail. ◆ Students apply scientific ideas to design, test, and refine a device to power their city, but are not always clear on how it works. ◆ Model and plan show evidence of research and planning, but not from a variety of sources.	◆ Plan demonstrates how energy will be distributed throughout the city but does not clearly show the benefits of the choice of power. ◆ The plan looks professional for the most part, but is not always realistic or clearly labeled. ◆ Plan gives an idea of how the city will be able to expand and grow but is not very clear.	◆ Model provides a general idea of how the city will be laid out, but it is not always clear how everything works. ◆ Model represents how energy will be distributed throughout the city but does not clearly explain the benefits of the choice of power. ◆ Model looks professional for the most part, but some aspects need work.

Product Rubric: City of the Future, *continued*

Overall	Research	Plan	Model
Needs Work (D–F)	• Students do not provide much or any detail as to how energy and fuels are derived from natural resources and how they affect the environment. • Students do not apply scientific ideas to design, test, and refine a device to power their city. • Model and plan show little or no evidence of research and planning.	• Plan does not demonstrate how energy will be distributed throughout the city and/or does not show the benefits. • Plan looks sloppy and unprofessional, and it is not clear what certain aspects represent. • Plan does not give an idea of how the city will be able to expand and grow.	• Model does not provide a clear idea of how the overall city will be laid out and how these elements will work together. • Model does not represent how energy will be distributed throughout the city and/or does not explain the benefits of the choice of power. • Model looks sloppy and it is not clear what certain aspects represent.

Project 6: Exhibition

7 Essay

Essays are often thought of only for use in language arts class, but essays can be used for any subject area concerning any topic. An essay basically asks a student to explain what she has learned in written form. You would think this would simply be a translation of what the student is thinking into words, but that is easier said than done. Many students have difficulty making this translation, so it is important to teach writing in all subject areas so that students become familiar with how to make this translation.

What It Looks Like

Essays have a basic five-part structure:

1. **Thesis statement:** This explains the purpose of the essay. It can be thought of as an introduction, but the thesis should be reiterated throughout the essay. It should be strong enough to be able to be backed up with three pieces of evidence.

2. **Evidence 1**: This lays out the evidence that proves the thesis with supporting details. This might be an example from the text (language arts), an example problem (math or science), or a citation of a specific event that backs the thesis (social studies).

3. **Evidence 2**: This is the same as Evidence 1, but with a second example.

4. **Evidence 3:** This is the same as Evidence 1 and 2, but with a third example.
5. **Conclusion:** This summarizes the main thesis and the arguments made. Lots of gifted students like to skip this step because they think they are just repeating themselves. It is safest to assume nothing about the reader and be as clear as possible.

Establish this pattern with students at the very beginning of the year by having them write about their favorite color. Students must choose a favorite color (their thesis), give three reasons why it is their favorite color (Evidence 1–3), and make a final argument for the color (conclusion). Reinforcement for valuable skills is always a good thing. Going over this simple structure can go a long way in providing you with clear essays.

Build Your Own Mousetrap

In this project, students will create a new mousetrap, one that captures the mouse without harming it, unlike the original model. They will first design the mousetrap and then build a working model that can capture a stuffed mouse. Their design must include instructions on how to create it, measurements, and needed materials. They will then write an essay, comparing and contrasting their mousetrap with the original design and evaluating which one is better and why.

Connections to NGSS

◆ 3-5-ETS1-1

Materials

◆ Project Outline: Build Your Own Mousetrap (student copies)
◆ Suggested Timeline
◆ Lesson: What Makes a Mousetrap Effective?
◆ Handout 7.1: Engineering Design Process (student copies)
◆ Handout 7.2: Tool Safety Tips (student copies)
◆ Handout 7.3: Testing Your Model (student copies)

- Handout 7.4: Structure of the Essay (student copies)
- Product Rubric (student copies)

Supplemental Materials

- Materials for students to build mousetraps (wood, cardboard, foil, cans, etc.)
- Tools for students to build mousetraps (hammer, glue gun, stapler, screwdriver, saw, safety goggles, scissors, level, duct tape, masking tape, wrench set, etc.)
- Tools for teacher use only (drill, X-Acto knife, saw, etc.)

PROJECT OUTLINE

Build Your Own Mousetrap

Directions: Technology must change to meet the needs of people. Could you imagine if we had never changed the original computer, which was so large it took up an entire room? You are going to revisit a classic design of a product and try to improve upon it.

You will create a new mousetrap, one that captures the mouse without harming it, unlike the original model. You will first design your mousetrap and then build a working model that can capture a stuffed mouse. Your design must include instructions on how to create it, measurements, and needed materials. You will then write an essay, comparing and contrasting your mousetrap with the original design and evaluating which one is better and why.

SUGGESTED TIMELINE

DAY				
1 Introduce the project and conduct Lesson: What Makes a Mousetrap Effective?	**2** Review the engineering design process (see Handout 7.1), and allow students to brainstorm ideas.	**3** Have students begin researching and designing their new mousetrap.	**4** Have students continue researching and designing their new mousetrap.	**5** Have students complete designing their mousetrap and select materials for their construction.
6 Review tool safety (see Handout 7.2) and have students begin construction.	**7** Have students continue constructing their mousetrap.	**8** Have students test and improve their mousetrap designs (see Handout 7.3).	**9** Have students finish constructing their mousetraps.	**10** Have students begin writing their essay (see Handout 7.4).
11 Have students continue writing their essay.	**12** Have students continue writing their essay.	**13** Have students revise and complete writing their essay.	**14** Have students demonstrate their mousetraps.	**15** Have students turn in their essays and mousetraps (see Product Rubric).

What Makes a Mousetrap Effective?

Have students analyze mousetraps (bring in models for the class to view or find images online). If you bring in mousetraps, you will want to disengage the spring so that the trap does not hurt anyone.

Ask: *What are the advantages of the original mousetrap design?* Possible responses include:

- Relatively cheap to purchase
- Can be put in small places such as next to the refrigerator or underneath a table
- By killing the mouse it guarantees it will not return
- Fairly simple design that is easy to manufacture
- Several traps can be placed around the house
- Both indoor and outdoor use

Ask: *What are the problems with this design?* Possible responses include:

- Kills the mouse, which can be messy and inhumane
- People could step on it and be hurt themselves
- Pets could go for the bait and have it snap on them
- Have to be set each time
- Can only catch one mouse at a time
- Could be dangerous around little children

There is a saying, "Invent a better mousetrap and the world will beat a path to your door." What do you suppose is meant by that? Possible responses include:

- Making an invention better can make it easier to use.
- Improvements are being made to inventions all the time.
- Inventing something could lead to fame and fortune.

Remind students that they are going to create a better mousetrap. Their mousetrap cannot hurt the mouse. This is known as a *constraint* or a requirement. Success will be measured by this constraint.

As students begin planning their mousetraps, distribute Handout 7.1: Engineering Design Process, and share the following tips for creating their designs:

- Use graph paper if possible (can also design on the computer).
- Use proper drawing tools (i.e., ruler, compass, etc.).
- Use a pencil for the initial drawing and then go over with pen.
- Color your model design.
- Include dimensions for the model.
- Label the different parts of the design, writing clearly in print.
- Make the design large enough for others to tell what it is.

Name: _____   Date: _____

HANDOUT 7.1

Engineering Design Process

Directions: Follow this process in order to create your mousetrap.

1. **Ask:** What is the problem? This is the essential question. How do you create a new mousetrap that captures a mouse without harming it?

2. **Imagine:** Brainstorm ideas of how such a mousetrap would work. You can imagine anything you want. Eventually, however, you will have to actually create this mousetrap, so any complex ideas or ones that require expensive materials will need to be reconsidered. Keep it simple.

3. **Research:** Make sure the mousetrap you are creating does not already exist. Although imitation is the sincerest form of flattery, in the scientific world it is also stealing. Make sure your idea is original. You also need to research what materials would work best with your model.

4. **Plan:** Take the idea in your head and put it down on paper. Sometimes compromises have to be made because what you thought just isn't as practical as it needs to be.

5. **Create:** Build it. Carefully consider the materials and tools that you need.

6. **Reflect:** Make adjustments to the design as needed. You may end up changing part of the design, using a different material, or even scrapping the design and starting over.

7. **Improve:** Throughout the engineering process, you will constantly find ways to improve your plan and mousetrap. After it is finished, you will need to test it to make sure it works. There might need to be improvements made at that point as well.

HANDOUT 7.2

Tool Safety Tips

1. Your teacher must supervise tool use at all times. Your teacher can assist with major tools, such as saws and drills.

2. Wear eye protection when sawing or drilling—even if you're just watching.

3. Dress appropriately by rolling up long sleeves, tucking in shirttails, and buttoning up shirtfronts so clothing doesn't get caught in the work.

4. Wear closed-toe shoes.

5. Tie back long hair for maximum visibility and safety.

6. Correctly and gently put down tools when they are not in use, and *never* run with a tool in hand.

7. Minimize distractions. Make sure you are paying attention to what you are doing.

8. Try not to get frustrated. Sometimes things do not go as planned. Be open to trying different approaches to accomplish what you want.

9. Keep cleanup in mind. You need to put tools back where you got them and make sure there are no scraps or mess on the floor or work area.

10. Do not play with the tools. If you are caught playing with them, you might lose the privilege to use them.

HANDOUT 7.3

Testing Your Model

Directions: To ensure the effectiveness of your mousetrap, you need to test how well it works. Consider the following questions.

1. Does the model work to capture the mouse?

2. Does the model harm the mouse in any way?

3. Does it work as you envisioned it?

4. Does it look like you envisioned it?

5. Do the model and the plan match one another?

6. Does the model seem sturdy and well built?

7. Can you repeat the demonstration over and over?

8. After demonstrating it, does the model stay together?

9. Are there different materials you could use that would make your mousetrap better?

10. Does the model meet the requirements of the rubric?

HANDOUT 7.4

Structure of the Essay

Directions: This details the basic outline of your essay about your mousetrap.

1. **Thesis Statement:** This explains the purpose of the essay. It can be thought of as an introduction, but the thesis should be reiterated throughout the essay. The thesis statement for this project would address how the mousetrap that you designed compares with the original mousetrap. In this section, you might want to describe how your mousetrap works to provide some background information.

2. **Evidence 1:** This lays out the evidence that proves the thesis with supporting details. In this case it should be a direct comparison with your newly designed mousetrap as compared with the original one.

3. **Evidence 2:** This is the same as Evidence 1, but with a second example.

4. **Evidence 3:** This is the same as Evidence 1 and 2, but with a third example.

5. **Conclusion:** This summarizes the main thesis and the arguments made. In addition, you need to make a judgment based on the evidence presented about which of the mousetraps is better. This judgment will need to be explained and supported.

Name: _____ Date: _____

PRODUCT RUBRIC

Build Your Own Mousetrap

Overall	Design	Model	Comparison
Excellent (A)	◆ Design includes clear step-by-step instructions on how to make it. ◆ Design is clearly labeled with measurements and parts. ◆ Design looks neat and professional.	◆ Model looks exactly like the design. ◆ Model is durable and built sturdily so it can last. ◆ Model works, trapping the mouse without harming it.	◆ Essay clearly compares the design with the original mousetrap. ◆ Essay presents both advantages and disadvantages of each trap. ◆ Essay provides exceptional detail and examples of how one trap is better than the other.
Good (B–C)	◆ Design includes step-by-step instructions but they are unclear, making the mousetrap difficult to reproduce. ◆ Design is labeled with measurements and parts, but some are missing or mislabeled. ◆ Design looks neat and professional for the most part but is sloppy in places.	◆ Model looks similar to the design with only a couple of minor changes. ◆ Model is durable and built sturdily for the most part, but there are parts that won't last. ◆ Model works for the most part, trapping the mouse without harming it, but there are several errors.	◆ Essay compares the design with the original mousetrap, but it is not always easy to understand. ◆ Essay presents advantages or disadvantages of the traps but not both. ◆ Essay explains why one trap is better than the other but does not include many details or examples.
Needs Improvement (D–F)	◆ Design does not include instructions of how to make it. ◆ Design is not labeled with either measurements and/or parts. ◆ Design does not look neat and professional, is sloppy and hard to understand.	◆ Model looks nothing like the design. ◆ Model is not durable and built sturdily; it won't last for more than a couple of uses. ◆ Model does not work or falls apart while trying to trap, or it harms the mouse.	◆ Essay does not compare the design with the original mousetrap. ◆ Essay does not present either advantages or disadvantages of both traps. ◆ Essay does not explain why one trap is better than the other.

8 Research Paper

One way to look at a research paper is as an expanded essay. Essentially, it follows the same structure: introduction of thesis, evidence, and conclusion. The big difference is that students are also responsible for conducting independent research. For an essay, the teacher often provides the background information or data for a student to be able to answer the question presented in an essay format. The students are merely synthesizing what they have learned from the teacher and communicating how it fits into the essay. The essay can be written on the spot and is a culmination of what has been taught. A research paper, on the other hand, has the students acquiring the information for themselves by using various sources, including books, the Internet, or interviews. The writing aspect is the last thing the student will be doing. There is the process of finding, evaluating, and organizing the information. Finally, the student must properly cite sources.

What It Looks Like

The key to a good research paper is providing an outline for students to follow. The outline can be very basic or it can be detailed depending on the level of the student. The outline should walk students through what is expected in the paper. Students should be able to use this as a blueprint to construct their research paper.

It is important for students to understand there is a structure to a research paper and that the outline is the backbone around which they will build the research. Once they understand this and have a solid outline, the creation of the paper becomes a matter of building it around the outline. This will make the writing of all future research papers easier.

Going to the Zoo

Could your zoo do a better job of making the animals feel at home? In this project, students will write a research paper about an animal at their local zoo. They will take a field trip to the zoo so that they can independently study the animal they are researching. Their end product will be a research paper combining online research with their personal observations of the animal.

Note. This project involves organizing a field trip to the zoo, but it could be altered so that students can complete the assignment in class.

Connections to NGSS

- ◆ 3-LS2-1
- ◆ 3-LS3-2
- ◆ 3-LS4-3

Materials

- ◆ Project Outline: Going to the Zoo (student copies)
- ◆ Suggested Timeline
- ◆ Lesson: Researching Your Animal
- ◆ Handout 8.1: Zoo Observations (student copies)
- ◆ Handout 8.2: Revising Your Draft (student copies)
- ◆ Product Rubric (student copies)

PROJECT OUTLINE

Going to the Zoo

Directions: Zoos have the tough task of making an animal most likely not native to the area feel comfortable. They have to make the animal feel at home so that it can adapt to its new surroundings. This involves mimicking the environment the animal comes from as much as possible. Could your zoo do a better job of making the animals feel at home?

You will write a research paper about an animal at your local zoo. You will take a field trip to the zoo so that you can independently study the animal you are researching. Your end product will be a research paper combining online research with your personal observations of the animal.

There should be five sections to your paper:

1. Introduction
   - What animal are you studying?
   - Why did you choose to learn about this animal?
   - What do you hope to learn?

2. Life cycle/habits
   - What is the primary food of this animal?
   - Where does this animal fall on the food chain?
   - What is the life cycle of this animal?
   - How does the animal's structure relate directly to its survival?
   - Does this animal form groups? If so, how large are the groups, and what benefits do they provide for survival?

3. Habitat
   - What habitat does the animal live in?
   - Which of the animal's traits make this a good habitat to live in?
   - What other animals live in this habitat, and how does this animal interact with them?
   - Do you think this animal could survive in a different habitat?
   - Are there traits that have evolved over the years due to the environment the animal lives in? What leads you to believe this?
   - How might changes in the animal's habitat be helpful or harmful? Use specific examples.

Project Outline: Going to the Zoo, *continued*

4. Observations
   ⋄ While at the zoo, what did you notice about this animal?
   ⋄ Did the zoo do a good job of setting up the proper habitat for the animal?
   ⋄ What improvements do you think could be made to the habitat to make it better for the animal?
   ⋄ What other animals are included in the exhibit and how do they fit with your animal?
   ⋄ Why do you think this animal is a good representative of the habitat the zoo has placed it in?

5. Conclusion
   ⋄ How did your research and observations of the animal complement one another?
   ⋄ What was the most interesting thing you learned about your animal?
   ⋄ If you could choose to live as this animal, would you and why?
   ⋄ How do you adapt to your environment? What examples can you provide to illustrate these adaptations?

© Prufrock Press Inc. • *10 Performance-Based Projects for the Science Classroom*

SUGGESTED TIMELINE

DAY				
1 Introduce the project and conduct Lesson: Researching Your Animal.	**2** Have students select an animal and begin research.	**3** Have students continue researching their animal.	**4** Have students continue researching their animal.	**5** Have students continue researching their animal.
6 Have students continue researching their animal.	**7** Have students conclude their research, ensuring they have all of the information they need.	**8** Have students begin writing their paper, following the project outline.	**9** Have students continue writing their paper.	**10** Have students continue writing their paper.
11 Have students continue writing their paper.	**12** Have students continue writing their paper.	**13** Have students continue writing their paper.	**14** Zoo field trip: Have students record their observations (see Handout 8.1).	**15** Have students continue writing their paper.
16 Have students continue writing their paper.	**17** Have students revise their papers (see Handout 8.2).	**18** Have students complete their papers (see Product Rubric).		

LESSON

Researching Your Animal

Selecting Animals

Direct students to the local zoo website. From there, they should be able to explore and identify animals they would like to study. Encourage students to select different animals. There should be enough animals for each student in the class to do a different animal. This provides more variety to the project.

Conducting Research

Now that students have identified an animal, direct them to research their animals online, answering questions on their project outline. (*Note.* If students need a lesson on conducting research, see Lesson: Conducting Research, p. 13.)

Encourage students to answer the questions on the outline using a lot of detail and examples. The more they find in their research, the more than can include in their research paper. You also will want to encourage them to find information from multiple sources. Consider meeting with students occasionally to check over their notes and ensure they are detailed enough for their purposes.

You have the option of having students include a works cited with their research paper. Make sure students keep track of their sources as they research, so that they can be credited when writing the paper.

Name: _____ Date: _____

HANDOUT 8.1

Zoo Observations

Directions: At the zoo, you will need to make your personal observations of the animal you are studying. This should not just be a reporting of the activities the animal is doing but also your reflections on why you think it is doing them. Add as much of your insight and thoughts as possible. Record your observations in detail.

1. What did you notice about your animal?

2. Did the zoo do a good job of setting up the proper habitat for the animal?

3. What improvements do you think could be made to the habitat to make it better for the animal?

4. What other animals are included in the exhibit and how do they fit with your animal?

5. Why do you think this animal was placed in this section of the zoo? How does it fit with the other exhibits in this section?

HANDOUT 8.2

Revising Your Draft

Directions: Edit your paper for correct grammar, spelling, sentence structure, and content, using the following tips.

1. **First Round of Editing:** Using the project outline, make sure everything is discussed and answered in detail. Read your paper, pretending you know nothing about your topic and this paper is teaching you everything you need to know about it.

2. **Second Round of Editing:** Using spell check is not always enough. You need to go through the paper and make sure things are spelled correctly and that the correct forms of words are used.

3. **Third Round of Editing:** During this round, you will want to find a place where you can read the paper out loud. This is a good way to check that your sentence structure is clear and that what you are writing makes sense. If you have trouble saying a sentence out loud, chances are a person reading it will also struggle. Fix these awkward sentences so that your paper makes sense and flows.

4. **Final Round of Editing:** Use the rubric as a checklist to make sure you have met all of the requirements of the research paper and that it is of the quality level you want it to be. If there are sections that seem to need improvement, what can be changed to get them into the excellent range?

Name: _____   Date: _____

PRODUCT RUBRIC

Going to the Zoo

Topic: _____

Overall	Content	Organization	The Why	Grammar
Excellent A–B	• Paper uses a lot of good information from a variety of reliable sources. • Paper uses detailed zoo observations that include the student's reflection. • Paper shows a thorough understanding of the topic.	• Paper follows a clear, logical order. • Paper follows the outline completely.	• Paper answers the "whys," providing complete information about the animal and its habitat. • Paper uses examples to illustrate points and includes lots of detail.	• Paper has few or no errors in spelling, grammar, or usage. • Sentences are organized and make sense, one leading into the next.
Good B–C	• Paper uses a lot of information from a variety of sources, but they are not all reliable. • Zoo observations are a play-by-play that do not include any student reflections. • Paper shows understanding of major points but limited understanding of details.	• Paper follows a clear, logical order but gets off track sometimes. • Paper follows most of the outline but some topics are not addressed.	• Paper answers the "whys" but does not provide complete explanations. • Paper uses examples to illustrate some points but lacks details in other areas.	• Paper has many errors in spelling, grammar, or usage. • Sentences are organized but are often choppy and do not flow together.
Needs Improvement D–F	• Paper does not use a lot of information and/or information from a variety of sources. • Zoo observations are minimal without much student reflection. • Paper shows lack of understanding about key points.	• Paper lacks direction or is confusing. • Paper does not follow the outline, leaving the paper incomplete.	• Paper does not answer many of the "whys." • Paper does not use many examples or lacks detail where it really can be used.	• Errors in spelling, grammar, or usage interfere with the meaning of the paper. • Sentences are not organized and there is no logical flow to the paper.

Project 8: Research Paper

9 Journal/ Student Log

Journals and student logs allow for a more informal style of writing. Although it is important for students to be able to write a proper essay, it is also important to give students the opportunity to be creative and not be constrained by the structure of an essay. Journals and student logs allow students to explore ideas without being tied to an essay format. The format need not even include complete sentences. Students can draw, write poetry, make lists, write letters from the perspective of another person, draw charts, or use any other form of expression.

Journals also do not need to be exclusive to language arts class. Students can journal in science, social studies, math, and even gym class. Journals show the progression of learning. Students can go back and see how much they have learned and what route they took to get there.

What It Looks Like

The nice thing about journal entries is that unlike an essay or research paper, which has a clear structure, there is more flexibility to look like whatever the teacher or student wishes for it to be. Journal entries usually start with a prompt. Writing prompts using higher level language allow for higher level thinking. It is important not to encourage lower level journal entries by assigning lower level prompts. Using key words from Bloom's

117

taxonomy to do this will help in the writing of these higher level prompts (Sedita, 2012).

Energy Around the House

In this project, students will draw a diagram of their home, identifying all major sources of energy in it. Then, they will identify a form of energy in sound, light, heat, and electrical circuits and research how energy is transferred in the process of using it.

They will record their observations and research in a science journal, noting how the source of energy is used in their everyday lives. They will ultimately choose the source of energy they feel is most important to their household and explain why.

Connections to NGSS

* 4-PS3-2

Materials

* Project Outline: Energy Around the House (student copies)
* Suggested Timeline
* Lesson: Energy Around the Classroom
* Handout 9.1: Journal Entry Prompts (student copies)
* Product Rubric (student copies)

PROJECT OUTLINE

Energy Around the House

Directions: Whether you know it or not, the application of science is all around your home in the form of energy. This can be something as small as a night light and as large as your furnace.

You are going to draw a diagram of your home, identifying all major sources of energy in it. Then, you are going to identify a form of energy in sound, light, heat, and electrical circuits and research how energy is transferred in the process of using it.

You will record your observations and research in your science journal, noting how the source of energy is used in your everyday life. You will ultimately choose the source of energy you feel is most important to your household and explain why.

SUGGESTED TIMELINE

DAY				
1 Introduce the project and begin Lesson: Energy Around the Classroom. Distribute Handout 9.1 (Entry 1).	**2** Discuss energy in the home and student responses to Entry 1.	**3** Discuss how energy creates sound (Entry 2).	**4** Have students research their responses in Entry 2 and complete Entry 3 in class.	**5** Discuss how energy creates light (Entry 4).
6 Have students research their responses in Entry 4 and complete Entry 5 in class.	**7** Discuss how energy creates heat (Entry 6).	**8** Have students research their responses in Entry 6 and complete Entry 7 in class.	**9** Discuss how energy creates electrical circuits (Entry 8).	**10** Have students research their responses in Entry 8 and complete Entry 9 in class.
11 Have students reflect on the importance of energy, complete Entry 10 in class, and turn in their journals (see Product Rubric).				

Energy Around the Classroom

Have students observe the classroom and identify sources of energy, such as overhead lights, computers, air conditioning/heating, projector, PA speakers, electric pencil sharpener, etc. With the class, draw a diagram of the room and identify all the major sources of energy used in the room.

Tell students that all of these are examples of sound, light, heat, and electrical circuits:

- **Sound:** PA speakers, computer speakers
- **Light:** overhead fluorescent lights, lamps, LCD projector
- **Heat:** Bunsen burner, hot plate
- **Electric circuit:** light switch, electrical outlets

Tell students: *Tonight you will need to draw a diagram of your home, identifying all the sources of energy in each and every room. After finishing your diagram, you will need to complete Entry 1 and be prepared to discuss your responses tomorrow.*

How Does Energy Create Sound?

An example in the classroom would be the PA System. How exactly does it create sound using energy, specifically electricity?

Sound works through vibration. Loudspeakers use this in order to project sound. At the front of a loudspeaker, there is a fabric, plastic, paper, or lightweight metal cone. The outer part of the cone is fastened to the outer part of the loudspeaker's circular metal rim. The inner part is fixed to an iron coil that sits just in front of a permanent magnet.

Electrical signals feed through the speaker cables into the coil. This turns the coil into a temporary magnet or electromagnet. As the electricity flows back and forth in the cables, the electromagnet either attracts or repels the permanent magnet. This moves the coil back and forth, pulling and pushing the loudspeaker cone and creating sound. Like a drum skin vibrating back and forth, the moving cone pumps sounds out into the air.

How Does Energy Create Light?

An example in the classroom would be the LCD projector. How exactly does it create light using energy, specifically electricity?

The image begins with a powerful light source. The LCD panels themselves do not emit any light and must be illuminated with a light source that is either in front of or behind the panel. In an LCD projector, the light source is usually a metal halide bulb similar to a car headlight. When the bulb is hooked up to a power supply, an electric current flows from one contact to the other, through the wires and the filament. Electric current in a solid conductor is the mass movement of free electrons from a negatively charged area to a positively charged area.

As the electrons zip along through the filament, they are constantly bumping into the atoms that make up the filament. The energy of each impact vibrates an atom.

A polarizing filter, lenses, and reflectors clean, focus, and aim the light toward a special mirror. The mirror creates a prism that makes red, green, and blue light, which are all brought together to project the image.

How Does Energy Create Heat?

An example in the classroom would be a hot plate used to heat experiments. How exactly does it create heat using energy, specifically electricity?

Some materials carry electricity well, others badly. The good carriers of electricity are called conductors, while the poor carriers are known as insulators. Conductors and insulators are often better described by talking about how much resistance they put up when an electric current flows through them. So conductors have a low resistance (electricity flows through them easily) while insulators have a much higher resistance (it's a real struggle for the electricity to get through). In an electric or electronic circuit, we can use devices called resistors to control how much current flows.

Resistors work by converting electrical energy to heat energy; in other words, they get hot when electricity flows through them. A typical heating element is usually a coil, ribbon (straight or corrugated), or strip of wire that gives off heat much like a lamp filament. When an electric current flows through it, it glows red hot and converts the electrical energy passing through it into heat, which it radiates out in all directions.

How Does Energy Create an Electrical Circuit?

An example in the classroom would be the light switch. How exactly does it create electric circuits using energy, specifically electricity?

In this diagram, the black wire is "hot" and carries the 120-volt AC current. The white wire is neutral. You can see in the figure that the current runs through the switch. The switch simply opens (off) or closes (on) the connection between the two terminals on the switch. When the switch is on, current flows along the black wire through the switch to the light, and then returns to ground through the white wire to complete the circuit. When it is off it blocks the current from being able to flow and thus the light cannot turn on.

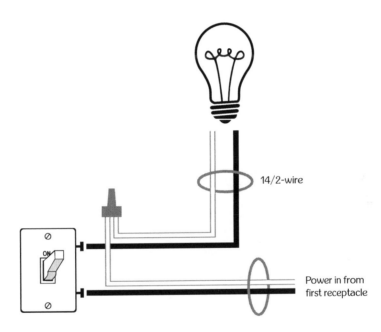

14/2-wire

Power in from
first receptacle

Name: _____ Date: _____

Journal Entry Prompts

Directions: Use the following prompts to write your journal entries.

1. **Entry 1:** Draw a diagram of your home. Label in each room the major sources of energy (this would include anything that is plugged into a wall outlet). Does the number of energy sources in your home surprise you? What do you suppose this says about your family's reliance on the transfer of energy?

2. **Entry 2:** Identify a source of energy in your home that uses sound. Describe why you believe this is an example of sound. What evidence leads you to believe this?

3. **Entry 3:** Research how sound is created in the source of energy you identified in Entry 2. Explain how the transfer of energy is what allows it to work. Draw a diagram demonstrating this transfer of energy.

4. **Entry 4:** Identify a source of energy in your home that uses light. Describe why you believe this is an example of light. What evidence leads you to believe this?

5. **Entry 5:** Research how light is created in the source of energy you identified in Entry 4. Explain how the transfer of energy is what allows it to work. Draw a diagram demonstrating this transfer of energy.

6. **Entry 6:** Identify a source of energy in your home that uses heat. Describe why you believe this is an example of heat. What evidence leads you to believe this?

7. **Entry 7:** Research how heat is created in the source of energy you identified. Explain how the transfer of energy is what allows it to work. Draw a diagram demonstrating this transfer of energy.

8. **Entry 8:** Identify a source of energy in your home that uses electric circuits. Describe why you believe this is an example of electric circuits. What evidence leads you to believe this?

Handout 9.1: Journal Entry Prompts, *continued*

9. **Entry 9:** Research how electric circuits are used in the source of energy you identified. Explain how the transfer of energy is what allows it to work. Draw a diagram demonstrating this transfer of energy.

10. **Entry 10:** Which of these transfers of energy do you feel is most important in your home? What examples could you provide to strengthen your choice? How would your home be different if it did not have this form of energy transfer?

Project 9: Journal/Student Log

Name: _____ Date: _____

PRODUCT RUBRIC

Energy Around the House

Overall	Content	Diagrams	Journal
Excellent (A)	◆ Explains with clarity, using detail and pertinent examples, how sound can be created through the transfer of energy. ◆ Explains with clarity, using detail and pertinent examples, how light can be created through the transfer of energy. ◆ Explains with clarity, using detail and pertinent examples, how heat can be created through the transfer of energy. ◆ Explains with clarity, using detail and pertinent examples, how electrical circuits can be created through the transfer of energy.	◆ Has a diagram of your home that shows several sources of energy that are clearly labeled. ◆ Has diagrams of sound, light, heat, and electric circuit that clearly show how they are created through a transfer of energy. ◆ Diagrams are clearly drawn/rendered and give a very clear idea of what they are supposed to represent.	◆ There are 10 detailed journal entries that address all the prompts. ◆ Produces clear and coherent writing in which the development and organization allows the reader to consistently understand what the writer is talking about in all journal entries. ◆ Journal consistently conveys ideas and information clearly by providing details and examples to illustrate points.
Good (B–C)	◆ Explains in a basic manner, providing an example to illustrate how sound can be created through the transfer of energy. ◆ Explains in a basic manner, providing an example to illustrate how light can be created through the transfer of energy. ◆ Explains in a basic manner, providing an example to illustrate how heat can be created through the transfer of energy. ◆ Exlains in a basic	◆ Has a diagram of your home that shows many sources of energy that are clearly labeled. ◆ Has diagrams of sound, light, heat, and electric circuit that give a basic idea how they are created through a transfer of energy, but links could be made clearer. ◆ Diagrams are well drawn/rendered but do not always give a very clear idea of what they are supposed to represent.	◆ There are 10 journal entries but a few are either lacking detail or do not address all the prompts. ◆ Produces clear and coherent writing in which the development and organization allows the reader to consistently understand what the writer is talking about in most entries, but a couple are difficult to follow. ◆ Journal conveys ideas and information by providing details and

Product Rubric: Energy Around the House, *continued*

Overall	Content	Diagrams	Journal
Good (B–C), *continued*	manner, providing an example to illustrate how electrical circuits can be created through the transfer of energy.		examples to illustrate most points but not all.
Needs Improvement (D–F)	◆ Either does not explain how sound can be created through the transfer of energy or does not include an example to illustrate it. ◆ Either does not explain how light can be created through the transfer of energy or does not include an example to illustrate it. ◆ Either does not explain how heat can be created through the transfer of energy or does not include an example to illustrate it. ◆ Either does not explain how electrical circuits can be created through the transfer of energy or does not include an example to illustrate it.	◆ Either does not include a diagram of your home and its sources of energy or they are not clearly labeled. ◆ Either does not include diagrams of sound, light, heat, and electric circuit or do not give a basic idea how they are created through a transfer of energy. ◆ Diagrams are not well drawn/rendered and it is difficult to tell what they are supposed to represent.	◆ There are fewer than 10 journal entries or there are many prompts not addressed or a real lack of detail. ◆ Does not produces clear and coherent writing with development and organization, making it difficult for the reader to understand what the writer is talking about. ◆ Journal does not very often convey ideas and information clearly due to lack of details and examples to illustrate points.

Project 9: Journal/Student Log

10 Portfolio

A student portfolio is a collection of materials that represents what a student learned. It may be something as simple as a folder containing the student's best work, along with the student's evaluation of this work. It may also be articles or work from other sources that the student has commented or reflected on. The length of the portfolio is determined by the teacher. The portfolio could be a snapshot of what the student learned during a brief one-week project, or it can be an ongoing evolution of how that student has improved over the course of an entire year. For instance, the first part of a portfolio might contain an essay the student wrote on the first day of class. The remaining content of the portfolio might show work 6 weeks in, 12 weeks in, or at the semester break. What can be seen throughout this process is how the student has improved and acquired new skills or knowledge. Conceivably, a portfolio could track the student's progress for an entire year and even longer. The assessment of a portfolio comes more from the student commentary than it does from the pieces she selected as part of the portfolio. This commentary can be as informal as a student jotting down an observation from a highlighted piece of text to a formal essay that sums up the entire project or semester. Either one of these can be used in the classroom as a performance-based assessment.

What It Looks Like

According to Melissa Kelly (2014), there are three main factors that go into the development of a student portfolio assessment:

First, you must decide the purpose of your portfolio. For example, the portfolios might be used to show student growth, to identify weak spots in student work, and/or to evaluate your own teaching methods.

After deciding the purpose of the portfolio, you will need to determine how you are going to grade it. In other words, what would a student need in her portfolio for it to be considered a success and for her to earn a passing grade?

What should be included in the portfolio? Are you going to have students put of all of their work or only certain assignments? Who gets to choose? (para. 9)

Is the Weather Report Always Right?

Meteorologists have a tough job. They have to try to predict something that is completely unpredictable. Sometimes they get it right. Sometimes they are way off.

In this project, students will follow the weather reports from two different sources. They will record the predicted weather in a journal along with the actual weather that they observe. After 2 weeks, they will collect all of the information, displaying it on a table and/or graphical display, and determine which of the two weather forecasts was more accurate.

Connections to NGSS

* 3-ESS2-1

Materials

* Project Outline: Is the Weather Report Always Right? (student copies)

- Suggested Timeline
- Lesson: How to Check the Weather
- Lesson: Recording Data
- Product Rubric (student copies)

PROJECT OUTLINE

Is the Weather Report Always Right?

Directions: Meteorologists have a tough job. They have to try to predict something that is completely unpredictable. Sometimes they get it right. Sometimes they are way off. As technology becomes better and better, meteorologists have become better at predicting the weather correctly. How accurate are they?

You will follow the weather reports from two different sources. You will record the predicted weather in a journal along with the actual weather that you observed. After 2 weeks, you will collect all of the information, displaying it on a table and/or graphical display, and determine which of the two weather forecasts was more accurate.

Parts of the Portfolio

1. **Section 1: Predicted Weather.** Record the predicted weather from two different sources for 2 weeks. Choose a local weather forecast and a national one. You must decide what information you want to pull from the forecast.

2. **Section 2: The Actual Weather.** Observe the actual weather that occurs during the 2-week period. Be descriptive, including details such as daytime and night-time weather, cloudy/not cloudy, temperature, rain/snow, weather fluctuations, and/or photos of the weather throughout the day.

3. **Section 3: Comparing Predictions.** Create tables and graphical displays that compare the two sets of predicted data. By doing so, you will be comparing and contrasting the predictions made by the two sources.

4. **Section 4: Comparing Actual Weather.** Create tables and graphical displays that compare the prediction versus the reality. This will show how accurate the predictions were as compared to the actual weather.

5. **Section 5: Comparing Over Time.** Does the weather you charted over the course of 2 weeks reflect the typical weather found in the season? What evidence do you have that indicates this? What is the normal expected weather for this season? What causes the weather to be as it is in this season?

Project Outline: Is the Weather Report Always Right?, *continued*

6. **Section 6: Conclusion.** Which of the two sources had the most accurate prediction? What evidence can you provide to back this up from your graphs and charts?

7. **Section 7: Reflection.** Are meteorologists correct in their predictions of the weather? Would you feel a lot of pressure if you were a meteorologist? How important is it that meteorologists get their predictions as accurate as possible? What could go wrong if they did not?

SUGGESTED TIMELINE

DAY				
1 Introduce the project and conduct Lesson: How to Check the Weather. Have students record weather prediction for Day 1.	**2** Have students record weather for Day 1 and prediction for Day 2.	**3** Have students record weather for Day 2 and prediction for Day 3.	**4** Have students record weather for Day 3 and prediction for Day 4.	**5** Have students record weather for Day 4 and prediction for Day 5.
6 Make sure students recorded weather and predictions form the weekend (Days 5 and 6). Conduct Lesson: Recording Data, and have students record weather prediction for Day 7.	**7** Have students record weather for Day 7 and prediction for Day 8.	**8** Have students record weather for Day 8 and prediction for Day 9.	**9** Have students record weather for Day 9 and prediction for Day 10.	**10** Have students record weather for Day 10 and prediction for Day 11.
11 Make sure students recorded weather and predictions form the weekend (Days 11 and 12). Have students record weather prediction for Day 13.	**12** Have students record weather for Day 13 and prediction for Day 14.	**13** Have students record weather for Day 14 and prediction for Day 15.	**14** Have students create tables and graphical displays to summarize their findings.	**15** Have students complete Sections 6 and 7 of their portfolios, reflecting on the project.

How to Check the Weather

To begin, share with students how to access the weather from various online sources. Share with students one of the day's forecasts that you accessed the day before. Ask students: *How do you think meteorologists predict the weather? Why would it be important to know the weather for the day? What season is this date in? What is typical expected weather during this season?*

Share with students the other forecast for the day. Ask: *How are they similar? What are the differences? Why do you suppose there are differences? How is the information presented differently? Which one gives you better information?*

Access the current day's forecast from the same two sources. Ask: *Where are they similar to the earlier predictions? Where are there differences to the earlier predictions? Why do you suppose there are differences? How is the information presented differently? Which one gives you better information? Which one gave a more accurate prediction?*

Note. The day before this lesson, access two different weather forecasts for your area, such as https://weather.com and your local news station's weather report. Save them to view during the lesson.

LESSON

Recording Data

Graphical Displays

A graphical display is just using visuals or symbols to represent items. For instance, looking at a weather forecast for a 2-week period, there are various visuals used that indicate information. Share with students an example of a 2-week weather forecast with varying symbols and weather types. Discussion questions may include:

- What do you think the symbol on (this day) represents?
- What about the difference between (this day) and (this day)?
- Which day seems like the best to do outdoor activities?

Tell students that the following are things to consider when creating a graphical display:

- Check your data.
- Label or explain encodings.
- Label axes.
- Include units.
- Consider your audience.
- Draw your graphical display with a straight edge when possible.
- Color also brings a graphical display to life.
- Have an appropriate title.

Tables and Graphs

Tables and graphs are just a method of organizing information so that it is easy to read. There are various kinds of tables. Share with students some examples of tables and graphs. Discussion questions may include:

- What is the information about?
- What is the range of (data collected)?
- How else was the data divided?

Tell students that in their weather tracking, they will need to decide the best way to display the information. It could be something as simple as a chart. Note that it is very important that a table contains a title and has parts labeled in order for someone looking at it to figure out what information the table is trying to provide.

Tables can also be used to make a comparison. If there are two sets of data measuring the same thing, they can be displayed in a graph that allows for comparison. For example:

Temperatures		
	Predicted	Actual
Monday	78	74
Tuesday	62	64
Wednesday	67	64
Thursday	64	62
Friday	71	70
Saturday	66	66
Sunday	69	67

A table that would compare these two would look something like this:

Temperatures in Fahrenheit This Week

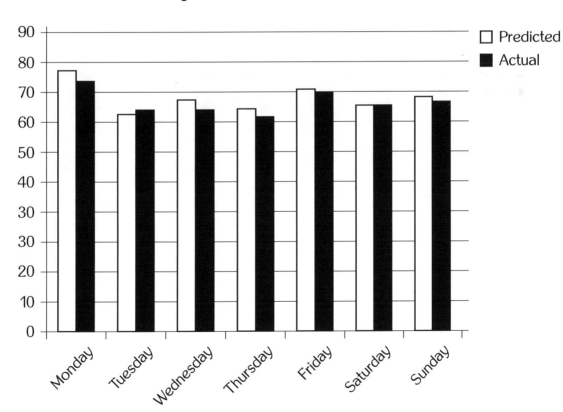

PRODUCT RUBRIC

Is the Weather Report Always Right?

Overall	Portfolio	Graphs/Tables	Content
Excellent (A)	◆ Portfolio is well-organized with all sections flowing into one another and easy to follow. ◆ Seven well-developed sections are included. ◆ Written sections use lots of detail and examples to illustrate the points being made.	◆ Graphs are clearly labeled and it is easy to tell the information being conveyed. ◆ A professional-looking set of graphs that organizes the predicted weather against one another, making it easy to compare. ◆ A professional looking set of graphs that compares the prediction versus the reality to making it easy to see the differences/similarities.	◆ Describes the typical weather in the season, why that is, and how the weather they observed compares with this in detail and with evidence. ◆ Conclusion compares the results versus the predictions and analyzes them using data from the charts/tables. ◆ Reflection is thoughtful and shares the feelings of the student using much detail.
Good (B–C)	◆ Portfolio is organized so it is easy to follow, but sections do not necessarily flow into one another. ◆ Seven sections are included but some could be more developed. ◆ Written sections use detail and examples to illustrate the points being made, but there are places where more is needed.	◆ Graphs are labeled and for the most part it is easy to tell the information being conveyed, but spots where it is difficult to tell. ◆ A well-drawn set of graphs that organizes the predicted weather against one another, but could look more professional, making it easier to compare. ◆ A well-drawn set of graphs that compares the prediction versus the reality, but could look more professional, making it easier see the differences/similarities.	◆ Describes the typical weather in the season, why that is, and how the weather they observed compares with this, but could use more detail and/or evidence. ◆ Conclusion compares the results versus the predictions but needs a deeper analysis of the data from the charts/tables. ◆ Reflection shares the feelings of the student but needs additional detail to make it more thoughtful.

Project 10: Portfolio

Name: _____ Date: _____

Product Rubric: Is the Weather Report Always Right?, *continued*

Overall	Portfolio	Graphs/Tables	Content
Needs Improvement (D–F)	◆ Portfolio is not very well-organized, making it difficult for someone reading it to follow. ◆ Less than seven sections are included or are so underdeveloped that information in section does not inform. ◆ Written sections lack detail and examples, making it difficult to figure out the points being made.	◆ Graphs are not consistently labeled, making it difficult to tell what information is being conveyed. ◆ A poorly drawn set of graphs that fails to organize the predicted weather against one another. ◆ A poorly drawn set of graphs that fails to compare the prediction versus the reality.	◆ Does not describe the typical weather in the season, why that is, and/or how the weather they observed compares with this. ◆ Conclusion does not compare the results versus the predictions or fails to refer to the data in the graphs. ◆ Reflection does not share the feelings of the student, making it difficult to understand what he or she learned.

Project 10: Portfolio

REFERENCES

Bastiaens, T. J., & Martens, R. L. (2000). Conditions for web-based learning with real events. In B. Abbey (Ed.), *Instructional and cognitive impacts of web-based education* (pp. 1–31). Hershey, PA: Idea Group Publishing.

Brydon, S. R., & Scott, M. D. (2000). *Between one and many: The art and science of public speaking* (3rd ed.). Mountain View, CA: Mayfield.

Dunn, R., Dunn, K., & Price, G. E. (1984). *Learning style inventory*. Lawrence, KS: Price Systems.

Grant, M. M., & Branch, R. M. (2005). Project-based learning in middle school: Tracing abilities through the artifacts of learning. *Journal of Research on Technology in Education, 38,* 65–98.

Haines, R. (2011). Fostering creativity and innovation in the science classroom. *Learn NC.* Retrieved from http://www.learnnc.org/lp/pages/7028

Horton, R. M., Hedetniemi, T., Wiegert, E., & Wagner, J. R. (2006). Integrating curriculum through themes. *Mathematics Teaching in the Middle School, 11,* 408–414.

Johnsen-Harris, M. A. (1983). Surviving the budget crunch from an independent school perspective. *Roeper Review, 6,* 79–81.

Johnston, D. E. (2004). Measurement, scale, and theater arts. *Mathematics Teaching in the Middle School, 9,* 412–417.

Jones, G., & Kalinowski, K. (2007). Touring Mars online, real-time, in 3-D, for math and science educators and students. *Journal of Computers in Mathematics and Science Teaching, 26,* 123–136.

Kelly, M. (2014). *Student portfolios: Getting started with student portfolios.* Retrieved from http://712educators.about.com/od/portfolios/a/port folios.htm

Kingsley, R. F. (1986). "Digging" for understanding and significance: A high school enrichment model. *Roeper Review, 9,* 37–38.

Ljung, E. J., & Blackwell, M. (1996). Project OMEGA: A winning approach for at-risk teens. *Illinois School Research and Development Journal, 33*(1), 15–17.

McMiller, T., Lee, T., Saroop, R., Green, T., & Johnson, C. M. (2006). Middle/high school students in the research laboratory: A summer internship program emphasizing the interdisciplinary nature of biology. *Biochemistry and Molecular Biology Education, 34,* 88–93.

Peterson, M. (1997). Skills to enhance problem-based learning. *Medical Education Online, 2*(3). Retrieved from http://med-ed-online.net/index.php/meo/article/view/4289

Renzulli, J. S., Smith, L. H., & Reis, S. M. (1982). Curriculum compacting: An essential strategy for working with gifted students. *The Elementary School Journal, 82,* 185–194.

Scholastic News Kids Press Corps. (n.d.). *How to conduct a journalistic interview.* Retrieved from http://www.scholastic.com/teachers/article/how-conduct-journalistic-interview

Sedita, J. (2012). *The key comprehension routine: Grades 4–12* (2nd ed.). Rowley, MA: Keys to Literacy.

Stanley, T. (2012). *Project-based learning for gifted students: A handbook for the 21st-century classroom.* Waco, TX: Prufrock Press.

Stanley, T. (2014). *Performance-based assessment for 21st-century skills.* Waco, TX: Prufrock Press.

Stewart, E. D. (1981). Learning styles among gifted/talented students: Instructional technique preferences. *Exceptional Children, 48,* 134–138.

Stoof, A., Martens, R. L., Van Merriënboer, J. J. G., & Bastiaens, T. J. (2002). The boundary approach of competence: A constructivist aid for understanding and using the concept of competence. *Human Resource Development Review, 1*(3), 345–365.

Toolin, R. E. (2004). Striking a balance between innovation and standards: A study of teachers implementing project-based approaches to teaching science. *Journal of Science Education and Technology, 13,* 179–187.

Trilling, B., & Fadel, C. (2009). *21st-century skills: Learning for life in our times.* Hoboken, NJ: Jossey-Bass.

U.S. Department of Homeland Security (2015). *Critical infrastructure sectors*. Retrieved from https://www.dhs.gov/critical-infrastructure-sectors#

Wagner, T. (2014). *The global achievement gap: Why even our best schools don't teach the new survival skills our children need—and what we can do about it*. New York, NY: Basics Books.

Whitener, E. M. (1989). A meta-analytic review of the effect of learning on the interaction between prior achievement and instructional support. *Review of Educational Research, 59,* 65–86.

ABOUT THE AUTHOR

Todd Stanley is author of seven teacher education books including *Project-Based Learning for Gifted Students: A Handbook for the 21st-Century Classroom* and *Performance-Based Assessment for 21st-Century Skills*. He was a classroom teacher for 19 years, teaching students as young as second graders and as old as high school seniors, and was a National Board Certified teacher. He helped create a gifted academy for grades 5–8, which employs inquiry-based learning, project-based learning, and performance-based assessment. He is currently gifted services coordinator for Pickerington Local School District, OH, where he lives with his wife, Nicki, and two daughters, Anna and Abby.

NEXT GENERATION SCIENCE STANDARDS ALIGNMENT

Projects	Next Generation Science Standards
Project 1	4-LS1-1. Construct an argument that plants and animals have internal and external structures that function to support survival, growth, behavior, and reproduction.
Project 2	5-LS2-1. Develop a model to describe the movement of matter among plants, animals, decomposers, and the environment.
Project 3	5-ESS3-1. Obtain and combine information about ways individual communities use science ideas to protect the Earth's resources and environment.
Project 4	3-LS4-1. Analyze and interpret data from fossils to provide evidence of the organisms and the environments in which they lived long ago.
Project 5	3-LS3-1. Analyze and interpret data to provide evidence that plants and animals have traits inherited from parents and that variation of these traits exists in a group of similar organisms. 3-LS4-1. Analyze and interpret data from fossils to provide evidence of the organisms and the environments in which they lived long ago. 3-ESS2-2. Obtain and combine information to describe climates in different regions of the world. 4-PS4-2. Develop a model to describe that light reflecting from objects and entering the eye allows objects to be seen.

Projects	Next Generation Science Standards
Project 5, *continued*	4-LS1-2. Use a model to describe that animals receive different types of information through their senses, process the information in their brain, and respond to the information in different ways. 4-ESS1-1. Identify evidence from patterns in rock formations and fossils in rock layers to support an explanation for changes in a landscape over time. 5-PS1-1. Develop a model to describe that matter is made of particles too small to be seen. 5-PS1-4. Conduct an investigation to determine whether the mixing of two or more substances results in new substances. 5-ESS1-1. Support an argument that differences in the apparent brightness of the sun compared to other stars is due to their relative distances from Earth.
Project 6	4-PS3-4. Apply scientific ideas to design, test, and refine a device that converts energy from one form to another. 4-ESS3-1. Obtain and combine information to describe that energy and fuels are derived from natural resources and their uses affect the environment.
Project 7	3-5-ETS1-1. Define a simple design problem reflecting a need or a want that includes specified criteria for success and constraints on materials, time, or cost.
Project 8	3-LS2-1. Construct an argument that some animals form groups that help members survive. 3-LS3-2. Use evidence to support the explanation that traits can be influenced by the environment. 3-LS4-3. Construct an argument with evidence that in a particular habitat some organisms can survive well, some survive less well, and some cannot survive at all.
Project 9	4-PS3-2. Make observations to provide evidence that energy can be transferred from place to place by sound, light, heat, and electric currents.
Project 10	3-ESS2-1. Represent data in tables and graphical displays to describe typical weather conditions expected during a particular season.